Praise for
Building a Successful Volunt
Finding Meaning in Ser
the Jewish Community

"Transmits the pragmatic wisdom that cultivates an inclusive and empathic guide for professional and volunteer leadership. Rabbi Simon's proactive mindset elevates the moral seriousness of boards and volunteers."
—**Rabbi Harold M. Schulweis,** Valley Beth Shalom, Encino, California; author, *Conscience: The Duty to Obey and the Duty to Disobey*

"Outstanding.... Highly readable and filled with practical wisdom on a topic that all Jewish professionals and lay leaders need to do their work more efficiently and more effectively. I intend to use this book again and again."
—**Dr. Erica Brown,** director of adult education, Partnership for Jewish Life and Learning; author, *Inspired Jewish Leadership: Practical Approaches to Building Strong Communities*

"Important insights about two of the most elusive populations in the contemporary Jewish community: volunteers and men. If there is one book whose insights can help save the postmodern Jewish community, this might just be it."
—**Dr. Kerry M. Olitzky,** executive director, Jewish Outreach Institute; coeditor, *Rituals and Practices of a Jewish Life*

"A thoughtful and thought-provoking book gained from more than thirty years in the field. A useful text for any communal leader."
—**Rabbi Michael Greenbaum,** vice-chancellor/COO, The Jewish Theological Seminary

"Filled to the brim with practical advice about how to tap the energy of volunteers and ignite participation in Jewish communal life. Rabbi Simon recognizes that Judaism is a 'contact sport' that requires more of its adherents than ritual observance."
—**Leonard Saxe,** professor of Jewish community research and social policy, Brandeis University

"Rabbi Chuck Simon understands what it means to motivate volunteers to bring about change in institutions. [With this book, he] has helped identify how to make our congregations institutions that can transform our communities and add deep spiritual meaning to our lives."
—**Rabbi Samuel N. Gordon,**
Congregation Sukkat Shalom, Wilmette, Illinois

"With deep empathy and fine insights, Rabbi Simon shows how to cultivate committed and caring volunteers. This is a necessary guidebook for developing leadership—and the best in human nature."
—**Francine Klagsbrun,** author,
The Fourth Commandment: Remember the Sabbath Day

"This easy-to-read volume contains numerous reflections, insights, and lessons that will prove valuable to anyone engaged in inspiring, mobilizing and managing volunteer leaders."
—**Steven M. Cohen,** research professor,
Hebrew Union College–Jewish Institute of Religion;
co-author, *The Jew Within*

"Shares remarkable insights about how culture affects both volunteers and staff, and how synagogues can cultivate volunteers and create leaders. I was particularly impressed with his careful analysis of the roles men and women take and how each can bring their unique strengths to synagogue life."
—**Rabbi Michael Gold,**
Temple Beth Torah, Tamarac, Florida

"Provides well-meaning people the practical skills needed to build an efficient and effective not-for-profit organization. Through its many specific suggestions and vignettes, this book gives us critical tools to transform our ideals into reality."
—**Rabbi Elliot N. Dorff, PhD,** Rector and Distinguished
Professor of Philosophy, American Jewish University, author,
The Way Into Tikkun Olam (Repairing the World)

Building a *Successful* VOLUNTEER CULTURE

Finding Meaning in Service in the Jewish Community

RABBI CHARLES SIMON

Foreword by SHELLEY LINDAUER
executive director, Women of Reform Judaism

Preface by DR. RON WOLFSON
president, Synagogue 3000

For People of All Faiths, All Backgrounds
JEWISH LIGHTS Publishing
Woodstock, Vermont

Building a Successful Volunteer Culture:
Finding Meaning in Service in the Jewish Community

2009 Quality Paperback Edition, First Printing
© 2009 by Charles Simon
Foreword © by Shelley Lindauer
Preface © by Ron Wolfson

Library of Congress Cataloging-in-Publication Data
Simon, Charles, 1949–
Building a successful volunteer culture : finding meaning in service in the Jewish community / Charles Simon ; foreword by Shelley Lindauer ; preface by Ron Wolfson.—Quality paperback ed.
p. cm.
Includes bibliographical references.
ISBN-13: 978-1-58023-408-5 (quality pbk.)
ISBN-10: 1-58023-408-9 (quality pbk.)
1. Voluntarism—Religious aspects—Judaism. 2. Voluntarism. 3. Corporate culture. 4. Leadership. 5. Boards of directors. 6. Committees. I. Title.
  BM538.V64S56 2009
  302'.14—dc22

2009018663

Manufactured in the United States of America
Cover Design: Tim Holtz

Published by Jewish Lights Publishing
A Division of LongHill Partners, Inc.
Sunset Farm Offices, Route 4, P.O. Box 237
Woodstock, VT 05091
Tel: (802) 457-4000   Fax: (802) 457-4004
www.jewishlights.com

CONTENTS

FOREWORD

In 1913, five thousand women gathered in Cincinnati to organize the National Federation of Temple Sisterhoods (NFTS). These women—all volunteers—understood the power of the collective to effect change in their local communities, in our country, and around the world. And bring change they did. Among their many accomplishments, our foremothers marched for women's right to vote, raised funds to build temples and schools, established social action committees, developed and led early childhood and religious school programs, initiated and funded the founding of the North American Federation of Temple Youth, and lobbied for women to be ordained as rabbis. They made sure the voices of women in Reform congregations were heard at the highest levels.

At a recent Reform Movement convention, Rabbi Eric Yoffie, president of the Union for Reform Judaism, told his audience of five thousand men and women, "When you want something done [in congregational life], get the women to do it." What was the power these five thousand women had that led NFTS (now Women of Reform Judaism) to eventually grow to a federation of six hundred women's groups representing nearly one hundred thousand women in North America? They had common goals, passionate spirits, the ability to reach out to community members, a plan for leadership growth and development, and the strength to combine all these elements into one dynamic organization.

Nearly one hundred years later, our congregations, our country, and our world have changed significantly. Women's organizations have faced membership and volunteer attrition over the past decade as societal and family demands on women have greatly increased. Questions about the necessity for single-gender organizations in an egalitarian movement are often heard. The opportunity for women to move directly into congregational leadership roles no longer necessitates the training and leadership development so long provided by sisterhoods. Philanthropic organizations with compelling missions and obvious need are vying for the limited time and attention of these valuable women.

So, where will we go from here? We follow the wise advice of Rabbi Charles Simon who, in this important book, brings us back to the essence of volunteer cultivation and engagement employed by the visionary women of National Federation of Temple Sisterhoods in 1913: articulating the organizational mission with passion, building community, incorporating our Jewish values—yet all within the framework of our current social and cultural environment. Rabbi Simon reminds us that volunteers are the bedrock of our not-for-profit world, our most valuable assets, to be nurtured, respected, and appreciated for their invaluable contribution.

SHELLEY LINDAUER,
Executive Director,
Women of Reform Judaism

PREFACE

Volunteerism is in trouble ... and Rabbi Charles Simon knows it. As the longtime executive director of the Federation of Jewish Men's Clubs, the male volunteer arm of Conservative Judaism, he has shaped a dynamic and engaged group of lay leaders, consulted with hundreds of synagogues throughout the world, and taught future communal leaders ways to increase involvement among those who would shape the spiritual communities of the future. In this insightful book, Rabbi Simon now shares his expertise with us.

Why don't people volunteer these days? Rabbi Simon correctly points out the usual reasons: everyone is busy with professional responsibilities, the demands of raising a family take priority, the frustration among those who desire to be "fast-tracked" to positions of power in organizations slow to develop leadership. I would add two other reasons people are hesitant to volunteer in synagogues: 1) if you volunteer to serve on a committee, there are so few volunteers that you are likely to be named the chair; and 2) it will be a "life sentence"—you'll never get out!

As in all "myths," as Rabbi Simon calls these factors, there is some truth here. But, to his credit, he goes much deeper to analyze why it is so difficult to recruit volunteers. With vivid real-life examples, he illustrates where organizations miss the mark by failing to adequately invite, engage, and appreciate laypeople. He correctly identifies the need to develop a *culture* of volunteerism in the organization.

In our work in Synagogue 3000, this issue of *culture* has been critical. Establishing such a culture begins with a "vision" of what the culture ought to be; in our case, we envisioned the synagogue as a sacred community—*kehillah kedoshah*. The core value in such a culture is viewing every individual as a human being "made in the image of God" —*b'tzelem Elohim*. Rabbi Simon casts a vision for an organizational culture anchored by the values of compassion, inclusion, flexibility, humanity, gratitude, fun, and trust. He skillfully guides the reader with examples of how these values can be operationalized in the development of a volunteer culture that works.

One word characterizes this vision of organizational culture: *relationships*. Rabbi Simon offers the example of his organization, the Federation of Jewish Men's Clubs, where the "culture of friendship" is paramount. The development of friendships depends on how relationships are cultivated, beginning with the nature of the initial invitation to volunteer and continuing through the lifecycle of engagement within the organization. One of the important contributions of this book is to help leaders understand that the relationships between clergy and frontline staff, between staff and laity, between veteran volunteers and newcomers, between board members and committee chairs, and between volunteers and the regular membership are human interactions that determine the quality of the volunteer experience. I have often advocated the need for synagogues and communal institutions that go beyond programs to create organizations where relationships are of highest importance. Programs will get people in the door—and may even get people to volunteer for short periods of time. But when the investment has been made to invite, establish, and cultivate relationships among people, the organization has a much better chance of expanding and retaining its volunteer corps.

Moreover, we need to know much more about the God-given talents, skills, and passions of those we seek to recruit. Most synagogues know very little about their members. The cutting-edge of volunteer engagement will rest on how well the organization can match a person's "spiritual gifts" and "passions" with the work that needs to be done.

Building sacred communities is itself sacred work. When you serve others, when you volunteer, you are doing sacred work. Rabbi Simon understands this and consistently brings us back to the notion that, although laypeople are motivated to volunteer for many disparate reasons, the most important is the awareness that the Jewish future depends on how we treat each other as we go about the business of creating our organizations. *Building a Successful Volunteer Culture* is an engaging and practical guide for our work, a must-read for professionals and laity seeking to build a healthy and effective volunteer culture.

DR. RON WOLFSON,
Fingerhut Professor of Education,
American Jewish University;
President, Synagogue 3000

ACKNOWLEDGMENTS

My wife and I moved to Paris in 2001. It was my first and, to date, only sabbatical. Mary left her job with a social service agency so we could have an adventure together. Never having that much free time before, I spent months thinking about how to fill it. I planned on seriously studying French, creating a second Masorti synagogue in Paris, and writing a book. My family really wanted me to write a book—a successful popular book. Yet I was at a complete loss about what to write. Every morning I woke up and devoted at least an hour to my writing. I wrote about the work I had been doing for nearly twenty years. I wrote about intermarried and soon-to-be intermarried couples. I continuously revised and reworked the material I had amassed during this period. I liked what I had written and found it humorous and engaging.

Upon returning home, the first thing I did was to go the local Barnes & Noble, gather every book on the shelves related to intermarriage, and skim them. I spent hours reviewing what had been written, only to learn that what I had written might be more humorous or a bit more insightful, but that I had nothing new to contribute to the literature.

Around that time, people began to realize that the Federation of Jewish Men's Clubs (FJMC) was a dynamic, growing organization while many others in the Jewish community were shrinking. FJMC invited me to speak about volunteerism and to assist them with board and staff trainings. I taught a few workshops with rabbinical students at The Jewish Theological Seminary. I began to accumulate lesson plans and notes from these experiences. A few summers ago, I began to transform my notes into essays and circulated them to interested parties, requesting comments and criticisms. I learned that these essays were changing the way volunteers and some professionals understood their organizations. That was the genesis of this book.

Special thanks to my wife, Mary, and son, Sam, who supported this project from the beginning. I would also like to thank Dr. Burton Fischman, Dr. Robert Braitman, my friends and colleagues who took the time to read the manuscript and share their questions with me; Stuart M. Matlins, founder and editor-in-chief of Jewish Lights Publishing; Emily Wichland, vice president of Editorial and Production at Jewish Lights, who in a very short time was able to transform *zuzim* made of copper into *dinars* made of gold; and a very special Jewish Lights editor, Ira Rifkin, with whom I wrestled and learned how to improve my work.

WHY RISK RAISING YOUR HAND?

Putting Volunteerism in Perspective

Volunteering isn't always easy.

How many times have people risked raising their hand only to have it figuratively slapped so hard it stung? I'd say almost as often as chicken is served at a Friday night Shabbat dinner. And how often has someone who is highly motivated indicated a willingness to volunteer only to be ignored? Perhaps not as often as chicken appears on the Shabbat table, but still far too often.

Volunteering definitely has its challenges. So does dealing with volunteers. Moreover, the challenges are completely different from those faced in conventional employer-employee relationships.

Volunteers are valuable commodities to any organization, but they need to be handled with care. They have limited time and are not necessarily interested in assuming leadership roles, regardless of how well they perform. People volunteer for different reasons, and executive-level not-for-profit professionals require specific talents and broad vision to weave together the different personalities and skill sets before them into a coherent, functioning volunteer culture.

In most cases, volunteers can't be fired. They are not business-world interns who can be dismissed at will. They are usually members of the community who have willingly come forward. Dismissing them inappropriately or alienating them can damage an organization's reputation in the community.

This book is about and for volunteers and the people who run volunteer-based organizations. My goal is to help them work together to create a successful volunteer culture.

TOYING AND JOYING WITH JEWISH LIFE

I have been an active volunteer and a professional analyzing volunteer-driven organizations for over thirty years. I have studied how religious and secular community-based organizations function, and I've studied large national and international organizations. I've worked with small, issue-oriented Jewish organizations, individual synagogues, and the international bodies of each of contemporary Judaism's major streams—Reform, Reconstructionist, Conservative, and Orthodox. I've analyzed Jewish Community Centers, camping programs, and local Jewish federations to discern what makes a successful volunteer organization tick.

Volunteerism builds relationships and communities. In my eyes, it is a core Jewish value that dates to Mishnaic (Greco-Roman) times. Volunteering broadens our worldview and helps make us better people. Key to this process is cultivating motivated volunteers and teaching those who run not-for-profits how to build healthy, vibrant volunteer cultures. Two incidents in my early career challenged and shaped my thinking about volunteerism and the organizations that seek to attract and involve volunteers.

Marketing Jewish Life

The first was a 1974 seminar organized for rabbinical students at The Jewish Theological Seminary in New York, where I was studying at the time. It featured Leonard Greenberg, a former co-owner of Coleco Toys, as the principal speaker. Coleco was the first company to produce a handheld video game. It was called Pac-Man, and it became an overnight sensation. The company followed up by marketing the Cabbage Patch kids doll collection, another major success.

Leonard's topic was "Marketing Jewish Life." The focus of his presentation was that we, as future rabbis, needed to understand the leisure-time market because we were in direct competition with it for the attention of our congregants. He explained that to attract people to our synagogues, we needed to develop a marketing strategy and view our successes as direct results of our sales efforts.

Sales efforts? Marketing strategy? The words sounded familiar, but seemed out of context. The few faculty members who attended the session were as baffled as their students. "You are teaching Torah, not selling hula hoops," they told us.

Leonard spoke a language that few of us understood. Yet it struck a chord. I remember one comment quite clearly: "The largest industry in Connecticut is life insurance, and they have a product that pays off after death. We have a product that pays off in life." I realized at that moment that if I were to be successful in my rabbinate, my thinking needed to shift from believing that a rabbi was a person who taught *mitzvot* to understanding that a rabbi was a person who marketed Jewish living.

Leonard changed my thinking. He inspired me to think, in effect, like a rabbinic marketing maven, someone who packaged, marketed, and delivered a product. He taught me that to appeal to my potential constituency, I needed to articulate why being Jewish and living Jewishly could enhance their lives in a way that made sense to them.

Infusing Passion into Judaism

The second incident occurred around 1982 while I was serving my second congregation. I was the associate rabbi and heir to a congregation in upstate New York. The congregation had approximately six hundred families and boasted a supplemental religious school of nearly three hundred children from nursery school age through high school. After I had served for a year, my senior colleague decided to take a long-deserved sabbatical and travel for six months. After nearly thirty years at the helm, he was finally confident that his congregation was in good hands. I was flattered.

A few weeks later, I began instituting minor changes. As an associate, I knew I couldn't tamper with major policies. But there were a number of smaller issues I felt could and should address. I began to consider Shabbat service attendance as a challenge and wondered how I might modify the service in small ways to create word-of-mouth buzz that might increase attendance over time.

I began to think of Shabbat services as a form of theater. My studies in liturgy had taught me that worship services in the Jewish world were viewed, in part, as entertainment. The best example of this were early Talmudic textual sources, indicating that the rabbis of the time extended the borders of what was permissible on Shabbat to allow more people to attend synagogue services, especially when a dynamic speaker was in town. It seems the rabbis understood that people attend religious services for a number of reasons, including entertainment.

I reasoned that almost everyone likes theater but that very few people enjoy bad theater—particularly if it is the same bad theater week after week. The Shabbat service at my synagogue, I concluded sadly, could be likened to bad theater.

Consider the following: At most synagogues the Shabbat service unfolds on a stage we call the *bima*. The services are well choreographed, include dramatic and less than dramatic moments, and are usually conducted by two principal actors, the rabbi and cantor. Supporting roles are filled by people who recite special prayers, and readings or are part of the choreography of the Torah service.

I began by modifying the choreography and eventually began to tweak the script.

One week, I changed a tune. The following week, I led a discussion instead of delivering a sermon. Once, the cantor and I successfully challenged the congregation to become active participants. It was a coup! Before the service we agreed that at a certain moment during the evening service I would interrupt his chanting and inform him in a disconcerted way that I was dissatisfied with how the service was going.

"Hazzan," I said, "I know you're trying, but this week, unlike other weeks, it's not working. I am not feeling the joy of welcoming the Sabbath. In fact, I am not feeling anything at all. Isn't there something else you can sing? Isn't there some way you can pull something out of your knowledge of Jewish music that can stir me?"

"Hazzan," I pleaded, "please do something!"

The congregation was shocked. I watched people nod to one another as a murmur began to rise from the congregation.

They agreed with what I said but couldn't believe I had said it. This was clearly a breach of synagogue etiquette.

The hazzan paused. He turned away from the congregation and scratched his chin. What an actor! We were doing pure theater.

Then he began to hum. He shook his head a few times and hummed something else. Slowly he turned toward the congregation, still humming and then chanting in a low, carefully modulated voice. He raised his head and started to pound his fist on his podium. We joined him. He built a rhythmic chant, and we sang with him. Before long the rhythm and the music lifted us to a place of true joy. The hazzan loved the charade, and together we moved the congregation from complacency to joy.

Other changes were instituted as well. I began teaching in classrooms, in the hallways, in people's homes, and at meetings with congregants at coffee shops. I created a lunch-and-learn Torah study group titled "You Can Be a Devout Jew and Not Believe in God." People who had never before considered studying with a rabbi began to attend my classes, including some non-Jews and Jews not affiliated with the congregation. Synagogue service attendance increased, as did the number of young people enrolled in our school and youth programs.

My small acts of rebellion—which seem so commonplace today but were nearly revolutionary back in the early 1980s—created a ripple effect. The synagogue was now growing and infused with a new passion. To meet the demands of an increased student body, I found myself recruiting new teachers, quite a challenge in a community two hours north of New York City.

I made lists of people who were minimally active in the synagogue but were engaged in what I considered interesting pursuits. They were academics, musicians, artists, lawyers, and shopkeepers. I called each of them and arranged to visit their homes. Most had only minimal knowledge of Jewish life and practice. Yet each possessed some skill that I needed. I asked them to volunteer, to take a chance. They accepted.

My meetings with these prospective teachers followed a pattern. Each was extremely flattered that I had taken the time to ask if I could be invited to their home to discuss a subject of importance. All were slightly nervous, because I had refused to explain over the phone why I wanted to visit. Every one of them flushed and hesitated to respond when I told them that I thought they were good communicators with skills and enthusiasm that could motivate young students from elementary school age through high school and that the community needed their talents. Finally, each agreed to take on the task because I was willing to take the risk along with them.

Leonard was correct. On some level each of these people believed that our product, Judaism, if properly taught, could make a difference. Once they overcame their initial fears, they were willing to take a risk because they believed in the product. They stepped forward to interact with Judaism in a new and exciting manner.

One man had an engaging sense of humor and loved film. I worked with him to develop a high school course on comedy in the Jewish world. I met with one woman who taught high school science. She agreed to teach the archeology of Israel. Every person I approached was flattered to be asked, hesitant to accept an unfamiliar role, but willing to try something new because I assured them that they were needed and could make a difference. Not one of them refused. Years after I had left that community, I learned that most of them continued to serve as volunteer teachers. A few ascended the congregational hierarchy and became synagogue presidents.

These two incidents helped me understand that people come forward to volunteer if they are approached in the right way—that is, if volunteering is marketed to them as a meaningful endeavor.

THE CULTURE OF VOLUNTEERISM

Unfortunately, too many not-for-profit organizations stumble along in a not-so-happy way, which results in bruised feelings, insensitive responses, and burnout on the part of volunteers and professionals. This book offers an alternative approach, viewing and analyzing volunteer organizations to help volunteers, lay leadership, and professional staff foster volunteer involvement and institutional effectiveness while minimizing the damage that often hampers the process.

This book is also concerned with deciphering the cultures of Jewish organizations. Just as there are slight cultural differences between Canadian Jewish organizations and their counterparts in the United States, so, too, do Jewish organizations differ from their counterparts in secular and other religious organizations. These cultural differences cannot be overlooked. Culture is the most fortifying factor of the organization. Failing to take an organization's culture into account can undermine the entire enterprise.

A number of years ago, while working in Europe, I attempted to create a satellite synagogue in Paris. The desired area for the satellite was three or four miles away from the parent synagogue and was strategically located closer to where a majority of the congregation's members lived. I assembled a group of synagogue leaders and requested a directory of synagogue members. I intended to establish a phone squad who would invite the members to services at the planned satellite location. A hall had been rented for the occasion. This seemed like a simple enough task, and my committee agreed to the plan. I couldn't imagine that it would fall flat.

Everything should have gone like clockwork. But in the end, the people who had agreed to work with me, who had seemingly bought into a plan that would help them, did nothing. At first I couldn't understand why they refused to cooperate with one another and with me.

And then I got it. Culture! The effort failed because I hadn't understood the culture of the French Jewish community. I had naively forgotten that the mayor in the designated satellite locale was a socialist, as were a number of our congregants. My undoing was that the leadership I had assembled belonged to different political parties. Capitalists and socialists don't always work well together. That seems obvious in retrospect. However, I had failed to realize that a call from the congregation president would be viewed by many as a political act. I simply did not understand the culture.

In the Christian religious world, cultural differences are even greater. American church culture is vastly different from Brazilian church culture, which differs greatly from Russian church culture, and so on. Even within American church culture you find tremendous cultural variation. Given that there are hundreds of Christian denominations in the United States alone, what else can we expect? The functioning and manners within various denominations and congregations may actually differ far more than those that divide Reform, Conservative, Reconstructionist, Orthodox, and secular Jewish organizations. Parenthetically, boards of directors and not-for-profit secular organizations like the Rotary Club closely parallel the way Christian religious bodies operate, because these organizations developed from the larger Christian culture. The only area in which I suspect that all volunteer not-for-profit organizations function similarly relates to the nature of nominating committees, which we'll discuss in chapter 7.

The Gender Factor

This book also includes separate chapters about the need for gender-based strategies when organizations are seeking to attract volunteers. While women, finally, are being allowed to take more leadership roles in the not-for-profit world, men, sadly, are increasingly less visible as volunteers. A recent study by Brandeis University professor Sylvia Barak Fishman clearly describes this situation:

> Within the liberal wings of American Judaism, women are increasingly prominent both as leaders and participants, and men are increasingly marginal. This gender imbalance differs from most Jewish communities historically and from many other Jewish communities around the world today. The systemic alienation of American Jewish males begins in boyhood, and has profound effects on every aspect of Jewish life. This development is of concern to Jewish leaders and policy planners because it affects not only religious but also communal and demographic realities. Jewish activities have less value, and Jewish friends and potential marriage partners seem less appealing to Jewish boys and men than they do to girls and women. (Sylvia Barack Fishman and Daniel Parmer, "Policy Implications of the Gender Imbalance amongst American Jews" in *Jewish Political Studies Review* [Fall 2008, Vol. 20], 3–4)

I believe this trend is reversible, but only if we learn to approach male involvement from the viewpoint of gender needs. This means changing strategies from those employed in the past.

Women, and the manner in which they are attracted to volunteering, also require different strategies when it comes to recruitment and retention. A number of international women's organizations are currently experiencing tremendous difficulty attracting new volunteers. Their volunteer bases are shrinking. This could be a result of the ways they seek to involve women, which must be revisited if they wish to meet the evolving needs of emerging generations. So we must adopt a gender-based approach to cultivating volunteers in the twenty-first century.

One last thought. We can never forget that volunteering is a two-way street. Volunteers must be motivated, but volunteer organizations also need to maximize volunteer satisfaction. Blaming one or the other for the failures prevalent today in the world of Jewish volunteerism helps no one.

The search is for a win-win strategy. Let's get started.

How Can I Fit In?

Deconstructing
Organizational Culture

Understanding organizational culture is the key to improving it.

Each year, I am invited to teach a number of classes at The Jewish Theological Seminary in New York. While the particulars of my classes vary from year to year, I always devote at least one session when teaching graduating rabbinical students to building commitment and fostering volunteerism. I begin my class with the statement that every not-for-profit organization is unique and that students can learn about the organization by viewing it as a separate and distinct culture.

For many years I always asked my class, "Do you understand what I mean by 'organizational culture'?" At that point, almost on cue, all the students would nod their heads in agreement. "Ah," I would think to myself, "these students are so smart."

In recent years, my thinking about organizational structure and the culture of volunteer organizations has changed, as has my style when working with not-for-profit boards. This change stemmed, in part, from an invitation I received to critique an organization's board training. The training consultant had lectured the board but had not, in my estimation, prepared appropriately or planned for follow-up. The insight I gained from this experience made me realize that my own presentations needed to be more engaging and more interactive.

So the next time I taught a class, I approached the topic in a more proactive way. Instead of simply asking a question and allowing a nod to inform me that I was being understood, I began by stating, "Let's make a list of the elements that comprise a not-for-profit or volunteer organization's culture. Who wants to begin?"

Silence. I looked at the group; clearly I was not providing them with sufficient information to come up with an answer. I tried another way.

"How many of you have a social circle of friends and acquaintances?"

Almost all of them raised their hands.

"Good," I said. "Substitute the word *culture* for *circle of friends*. Can anyone suggest any of the elements that keep your culture together?"

And then we began to make a list.

CORE MYTHS: THE BIG STORY

The first question to ask when you're attempting to define an organization's culture is this: What is its core myth? Every organization is founded on a core myth, or master story. By "myth" I mean a basic truth or belief that strengthens an organization and gives it direction. A core myth is how an organization views itself and wants to be viewed by outsiders.

Judaism's two great core myths are the Exodus story and the experience at Sinai. These are the stories around which our peoplehood, our religion, and our way of life have coalesced. A synagogue or a school that wants to be viewed as personable, warm, and intimate will seek to attract people who are looking for warmth and intimacy. If it projects that image to its members and potential members through its activities and written and spoken messages, that story will spread to the community at large.

The image might not reflect the reality. It might actually only be a goal or a desire, but if the leaders of that synagogue or school promote that idea, undoubtedly it will spread.

Some institutions have no interest in creating a warm and friendly atmosphere. Instead, they strive to cultivate a more structured atmosphere, where emotional distance and formality hold sway.

The Reform Movement began in the early nineteenth century in Germany, modeling itself after the worship style of the era's dominant Protestant churches. As a result, Reform created a formal worship culture. In one example of that formality, Reform rabbis officiated from a stage located in front and separate from the congregation, rather than in its midst, as was the prevailing Orthodox norm.

> Every organization is founded on a core myth, or master story. A core myth is how an organization views itself and wants to be viewed by outsiders.

The new model was a tremendous success because it signaled to those dissatisfied with Orthodox Judaism that Reform was rejecting the past for a new path forward. So an atmosphere that cultivates distance and hierarchy can also work.

As the times changed and congregations affiliated with the Reform Movement sought to grow and attract members of the younger generation, they began a process of repositioning, modifying the myth of who they are and changing the manner in which they were perceived. In the 1960s, informal worship services began to replace the formal arrangement that originally helped define the Reform Movement, and guitars began to replace the more formal choirs. The ramifications of these modifications were far-reaching and successful.

An organization that strives to reach out to other community-based organizations—to join with them to effectively implement local projects—embodies a core belief that people working together can change a community. Core myths/beliefs are not economically driven, though they may result in financial gain, depending on how the organization structures its fundraising.

This also is true in the for-profit sector. For example, the core myth cultivated by the Disney Corporation is that it is *the* destination for a fun-filled, family experience.

Core myths or beliefs should not be confused with core values. A core value supports the myth, the mission of the organization. Core values, such as providing food for the hungry and jobs for the unemployed, are examples of the components that unite people in common purpose. People whose core values are different from those of the institution often face a dilemma that affects how they operate as volunteers. They have a choice. They can embrace the organization's core values, or if this is not possible, they can choose to volunteer elsewhere. Not every organization is suitable for every volunteer.

Take a woman who volunteers in a community-based organization and enjoys everything from stuffing envelopes to delivering food baskets. She might be appropriately paired with a not-for-profit organization that strives to feed the hungry. If she were more comfortable raising funds than visiting a soup kitchen, she might be better off volunteering with a different type of organization. Some people prefer to become active in an organization that is more hierarchical and better staffed, while community-based volunteers might think that this kind of organization fails to reflect their core values. Lay leaders and professionals have to recognize that talent is not always transferable, that everyone is not suited for every task in every setting.

Engaging and developing talent requires the right opportunity and the right organizational culture. It is crucial to find the right people to help transform an organization into one that best reflects its mission and overall purpose.

COMING TOGETHER WITH COMMON LANGUAGE

A central component of the core myth is common language. A common language unites people in purpose and continuously reinforces the organization's mission. A common language is composed of key phrases that inform the potential volunteer or community member about why the organization is important and what it can do for the volunteer and the targeted service community. A common language resonates, attracts, motivates, and involves. A common language should be inclusive, even if an organization is exclusive.

> Talent is not always transferable. Not everyone is suited for every task in every setting.

For a common language to be successful it needs to be employed regularly by institutional leaders. Key phrases should be repeated in print, sermons, and lectures. The common language must be consciously articulated for it to be ingrained in the leadership's collective unconscious. The language reinforces the institution's core myth. For example, to cultivate a "caring" institutional image, the word "caring" and a number of its synonyms must become part of the institution's everyday vocabulary. A well-crafted common language provides membership and potential membership with reasons to support the organization.

The first time I witnessed a common language reinforcing the core myth of an institution was a number of years ago when I visited a major synagogue in Texas. Over the course of several days, I had a number of opportunities to listen to the founding rabbi, a gentleman who had been with the synagogue from the early 1940s and was approaching retirement, along with his two assistants. I also interviewed a number of the synagogue's lay leaders, active and nonactive members, and staff.

One Friday evening I attended services and heard the rabbi preach. He used the phrase "the survival of the Jewish people" twice during the course of his sermon. The following day I heard the same phrase repeated by each of his two assistants under different circumstances. Later in the weekend I heard the phrase uttered by staff members and lay leaders during the course of normal conversation. Clearly, members joined this particular synagogue and participated in its activities because they were concerned about the "survival of the Jewish people."

> A culture of friendship is created through a process that constantly challenges the leadership to interact with people on emotional and personal levels. This isn't easy.

The core myth of the Federation of Jewish Men's Clubs (FJMC), the male volunteer arm of Conservative/Masorti Judaism, is "involving Jewish men in Jewish life." One of FJMC's core values is "respect for one another." Another is "We need to challenge each other and be challenged to live more meaningful Jewish lives." FJMC strives to accomplish this through language by speaking of a "culture of friendship."

This culture is created through a process that constantly calls on its leadership to interact with people on emotional and personal levels, instead of in the task-related ways common to many not-for-profits. This isn't easy. It means that leaders need to be taught to speak from their hearts.

Imagine the salesperson who begins an interview or sales pitch by asking prospective clients about their family, children, and community before sharing information about his own experiences and before attempting to be of assistance or to close a sale. Physical actions like hugging, kissing, and offering people a firm handshake reflect the way nonverbal language can reinforce a culture of friendship. That is why FJMC trainers are taught to "hug."

One of the reasons people seek to become and remain active in FJMC is because they have been embraced by a "culture of friendship." Common language supported by specific gestures is a key component of a vibrant organizational culture.

WHO WORKS FOR WHOM?

The culture of organizations and institutions is reflected in the staff-volunteer relationship. Organizations can be professional staff–driven, lay-driven, or a combination of the two. If the organization is staff-driven, the professional staff make most of the primary decisions and view themselves as the institutional catalyst. That scenario places the core myth at risk, and it threatens to limit the number of volunteers in the organization. Yet if the organization is lay-driven, senior staffers may be placed in a subservient position, which cramps their style and limits their ability to bring their skills and talents to bear on the tasks at hand.

Two different perspectives that attempt to describe the most effective way to build an organization are currently in play in the not-for-profit community. The majority view posits that the most productive way to create community is to engage professionals.

The minority view holds that because community members are most invested in community outcomes, community organizations should be built by and around them. Both are partially correct.

The second perspective is a less expensive model for community development, but it is much more time-consuming. Ultimately, it can produce more committed volunteers and more fully maximize the strengths of lay and professional leadership. Under this framework, professionals are viewed as facilitators, guides, and motivators and, in that capacity, they are responsible for the creation of a partnership from which the core myth emanates.

Yet the number of people staff can motivate is limited. Staff-motivated institutions often fail to recognize that lay leadership is more strategically placed and can have a greater impact on larger numbers than can their professionals. An empowered lay leader, even one whose talents are more limited than those of a professional, has the greater ability to inspire, motivate, and impress others.

Staff-driven organizations have a tendency to underinvolve volunteers and to view them as "rubber stamps" rather than a source of vitality, renewal, and growth. They do themselves and their volunteers a disservice by failing to utilize the marketing and analytical skills of their volunteers.

I remember a phone call I received from one of the more active men's club chapters. The chapter successfully involved several hundred men on a weekly basis. These men fulfilled a number of important functions in their synagogue during the course of the year. They served as ushers, ran blood drives, raised funds, provided informal education, and were the driving force behind a host of social action initiatives. But club members were upset because the rabbi was undermining one of their efforts—sending club members into the afternoon religious school to teach shofar blowing.

I called the rabbi and asked why he was spending time on a function that volunteers were already fulfilling. His response was that it was easier for him to walk in at his leisure and teach the children for ten to fifteen minutes a day, two or three times a day, over the course of a week than to make the necessary phone calls to coordinate the scheduling of volunteers. The rabbi, who could have had his secretary make the calls, inadvertently alienated several hundred volunteers because it was "easier to do it himself." The staff-driven institution that fails to utilize the skills of its lay leadership creates a distance between lay leadership and staff members that can inhibit cooperation, create ill will, and seriously compromise the overall functioning of the organization.

> The culture that permits and fosters elitist attitudes performs a disservice and risks promoting individual aggrandizement rather than a team effort that pursues long-term objectives in a systematic way.

Structure Dictates Culture

Understanding how an organization is structured can reveal a great deal about its culture. For example, a major organization within the Conservative Movement created a regional presidents council several decades ago. When I questioned its purpose, I was told it had been created to serve as a counterbalance to the New York office, that is, the movement's East Coast leadership. In one sense, this regional council could be viewed as a means of soliciting more input from those in regions distant from the central office. It could also be interpreted as a reflection of how the central office and administration were viewed by their constituents.

A closer look at the bylaws of this organization reinforced the view that the council took a distinctly negative view of the

New York leadership. The bylaws did not prepare the ground-work for a smooth transition of leadership of administrations; instead, the organization was structured to ensure that the incoming lay president would not be designated until just six months prior to election. The structure of the organization was based on mistrust and, as a result, created a situation that got in the way of any long-term planning.

This approach is in direct contrast with another organization that nominates a first vice president two years before she assumes the presidency. The former example prohibits an incoming leader from developing a long-range agenda and putting together a leadership team. The latter organization, taking a wiser approach, allows appropriate time for thinking, planning, and assembling a new leadership team as well as ensuring that a smooth leadership transition occurs.

A healthy organization also provides its incoming leadership with ample opportunity to retain people who will not be nominated for the same or higher office, treating them in a dignified manner. Healthy volunteer organizations need to be cognizant of the emotional needs of volunteers who, in effect, come up against a glass ceiling and will not continue to advance as they may wish. Providing them with the opportunity to continue to serve is vital. Volunteers are our lifeblood. They should not be discarded in a callous manner.

The Drive for Legacy

Synagogues and organizations are often subject to the desires of their leadership to "leave a mark." These desires, while often well meaning, are not always in sync with the organization's needs or goals. This drive to leave a legacy is also an indicator of the organization's culture and should be viewed as a potential obstacle that needs to be overcome. While this kind of legacy building is hardly abnormal and is often considered acceptable behavior, the desire for legacy creates a project mentality that can inhibit long-range planning and teamwork. Each administration needs to assume the aims and goals of its predecessors. Words like "projects" need to be replaced with long-term words like "initiatives." The project mentality encourages a zigzagging approach to organization building.

The Role of Senior Staff

Senior professional staff must ensure that these types of attitudes do not prevail in the volunteer culture. They smack of elitism and are characterized by a language of ego ("This will be my project"). The culture that permits and fosters these attitudes performs a disservice and risks promoting individual aggrandizement rather than encouraging a team effort that pursues long-term objectives in a systematic way.

Senior staff need to anticipate and respond to the desires of new administrations with a language that builds from one administration to another. In working through this transition, staff must reassure the incoming president that he will encounter more than enough new ventures through which he can shape the organization's future.

ARE GOALS BEING MET?

Another indicator of organizational culture is how frequently an organization reexamines its constituent parts to ensure that its goals are being met. I am aware of several prominent religious organizations that have sponsored annual conventions for more than sixty years. The conventions typically run for four days and attempt to fulfill the needs of a growing constituency with diverse interests. For unknown reasons, the number of convention attendees has been consistent or has diminished in the past decade. The organization that examines its convention structure every few years would see this as a cause for concern. After all, a growing organization should have increased convention attendance if it is meeting members' needs.

I had occasion to question one of the organization's professional leaders about its stagnant convention attendance. I suggested that a less-expensive convention site or an alternate date might result in increased attendance. I was told in response, "This is what our people want. We did a survey last year, and everyone who responded to the survey wanted us to continue what we have been doing."

"That's very interesting," I said. "How many members do you have in the organization?"

"Fifteen hundred," was the reply.

"And how many people regularly attend the convention?" I asked.

"Three hundred," was the reply.

"I see. And how many responses to the questionnaire did you receive?"

"Three hundred."

Further questioning revealed that the three hundred respondents were more or less the same three hundred who came to the convention.

Reevaluating an organization's regular activities to determine if goals are being met is a positive indicator of a healthy culture.

BOARD OR BORED CULTURE?

The manner in which committee and board meetings are conducted also reflects an institution's culture and represents one of the greatest challenges to institution building. In the corporate world, people follow standard protocols in committee and board meetings to preserve their professional standing and improve their professional future. Similarly, committee and board meetings tend to be goal-directed and concentrate on maximizing time and productivity. People who fail to adhere to these rules risk failure and job loss. In the volunteer world, the rules are different. Volunteers don't lose their livelihood if they act in an inappropriate manner.

Consider how members interact during meetings. Do they follow established protocols? Are they respectful of one another when speaking? Do they bicker, interrupt, shout, claim personal privilege, or become easily distracted? Do they understand the difference between working in committee and sitting on a board?

There is an apocryphal story told about a Jewish organizational leader that makes a strong statement about organizational culture. The leader wanted to organize a rowing team and decided that the best way to get started was to dispatch a rabbinical student to Cambridge to observe how Harvard's team operated. He was a spy sent to learn their secrets.

Our young student traveled to Massachusetts, watched the team for some time, and then returned to his organization. He was quickly ushered into the leader's presence.

"What's their secret?" the leader demanded.

"Well," the rabbinical student said, responding slowly. "It was very interesting. They had one leader and nine followers."

The importance of clear lines of authority and teamwork could not be made clearer.

MODELING

A final indicator of organizational culture is how leadership models itself. Effective professionals and lay leaders model the behavior they wish others to follow. If the core myth of the organization encourages people to be more compassionate, then its leadership needs to model compassion. A leader—whether lay or professional—who takes the time to make a phone call or visit an ailing member has an impact that far exceeds the time invested. Modeling sets an example, deepens commitment, and builds teams.

Talking Points

• How does the culture of your organization support its core myth?

• How would you describe the common language of your organization? How could it be improved?

• What is the nature of the volunteer-staff relationship in your organization? Is your organization staff-driven or volunteer-driven? Have you forged a vibrant partnership between the two?

• Is there a gap between board and staff at your organization? If so, how would you close that gap?

• How would you characterize your board and committee meetings? Are they congenial, serious, and focused or mired in politics and easily thrown off course?

• Do any of your leaders "model" organizational values on a consistent basis? How could you encourage others to follow that example?

2

FROM BABEL
BACK TO EDEN

Creating a Language
of Inclusion

Human culture is revealed by language. The impact of what we say and how we say it is apparent in the facial and bodily reactions of those we address. By the same token, what we hear from others profoundly affects how we function in relationship to them. This is why language, our everyday vocabulary, is so important to creating and sustaining Jewish institutions that rely on a solid base of volunteers.

Institutions create a language of self-definition. This lexicon—often unconscious, sometimes consciously chosen—is established by leaders and folded into daily usage when transmitted from staffer to staffer, volunteer to volunteer. When the language resonates or taps a cultural chord, it spreads rapidly. In recent decades, words like "awesome" and "cool" have become an integral part of the lexicon. Consider

> The role of language, our everyday vocabulary, is important to creating and sustaining Jewish institutions that rely on a solid base of volunteers.

that twenty years ago a person who elected to become Jewish was labeled "a convert." Today, as a result of the conscious effort of a few people who were in the forefront of the movement to make widespread conversion both accessible and acceptable, the preferred term is "Jew by choice."

In addition to overseeing the management of physical facilities, Jewish organizational leaders are charged with providing a host of intangible services. These include stimulating people spiritually, attracting unaffiliated Jews, and bringing the community together for a prolonged and serious discussion of its future course. The fulfillment of this mission is complex and needs regular reinforcement. Why? Primarily because the forces that bound our communities together a century ago have so frayed that they no longer attract and involve people in the same way. In response to this change, our communities have developed membership committees, welcoming committees, caring committees, and outreach committees, all of which make people feel more welcome in the congregation or organization. All too frequently, organizations manage to involve large numbers of volunteers in a variety of activities but fail to inspire them to become part of their sales force, as Leonard Greenberg might put it, simply because they don't know how to employ inclusive, mission-centered language.

INCLUDE ME OR EXCLUDE ME?

People are motivated to volunteer based on whether they feel included or excluded, and that feeling arises from exclusionary or inclusionary language. The Orthodox world generally has a very engaged population, many of whom frequently volunteer within that community. The language of Orthodox culture employs words like "commanded," or the Hebrew terms *mitzvah* (commandment), *Halachah* (law), or *chiyuv* (legally obligated). Orthodox culture is exclusionary in that it insists that those who wish to enter adhere completely to Orthodox cultural norms.

The non-Orthodox and secular streams clearly favor more inclusionary language and fewer boundaries. There are always some boundaries; parameters are necessary for an organization to define itself and its mission. One way professional and senior volunteer leadership can help an organization to grow is by consistently using either inclusionary or exclusionary language that supports the organizational mission.

If the mission of the organization is to attract and involve people and to deepen their commitments, then a language that resonates, attracts, motivates, and involves—a language of inclusion—is preferable. Inclusive language is guided by the mission that defines and unites a community. I know of a synagogue in northern New Jersey that will only accept members if they subscribe to the *Wall Street Journal* and are able to read Hebrew fluently. This might be a wonderful community for some, but it was built on exclusionary language. Serious non-educated Jews may not apply.

THE LANGUAGE OF INCLUSION IN VOLUNTEERISM

Appropriately phrased and communicated, a language of inclusion can dissolve the fears and awkwardness that a prospective volunteer might harbor. It also strengthens the bonds between a member or prospective member and the community's vision. The organization that strives to develop the use of appropriately phrased language opens the door to spiritual, educational, social, and community concerns that need to be addressed. The synagogue that advertises itself as "a caring community" or as "your spiritual home" is making a strong overture to prospective volunteers.

When leaders communicate to volunteers, the tone of the language and the specific vocabulary used affect how their message is received. The message can be inviting and engaging or alienating and impersonal.

For not-for-profit organizations to meet the challenge of changing motivations and demographics, Jewish communities must understand that they are in direct competition with the leisure-time market. As a result, specific phrasing needs to be developed that will motivate people to embrace the product—Jewish community life—as well as reinforce community values and motivate people to do their part, to make a difference, to volunteer.

> People are motivated to volunteer depending on whether they are attracted to exclusionary or inclusionary language.

So how do we begin? Community leadership (lay and professional) must first have a realistic understanding of the nature, habits, and characteristics of their institution's current and potential membership.

John was attracted to a particular Conservative synagogue because he found the nature of the Torah dialogue on Shabbat morning stimulating. He barely remembered his bar mitzvah and considered himself a nonpracticing Jew. But this place felt good to him. He was attracted to the values the community espoused. He liked the Torah discussion so much that he didn't think twice about taking a pen out of his pocket and jotting down some notes based on what the rabbi was saying. John was a prospective member—until suddenly someone tapped him on the shoulder. "We don't do that on Shabbat," said a participant sitting nearby. "We don't write, at least not in synagogue."

Not a welcoming feeling.

Or take Sarah's case: It never occurred to her that she was violating a community value when she brought processed food to a community potluck dinner. She hadn't realized that community potluck dinners were organic and vegetarian because no one had told her.

WHO IS THE PROSPECTIVE CLIENT?

Community leadership needs to acknowledge that many members and potential members simply do not know the rules, so they must be explained in a simple, nonjudgmental way. This minimizes damage, avoids hurt feelings, and reinforces openness and opportunities for inclusion.

A language of inclusion transforms negative reactions from longtime members familiar with the rules, such as those directed at John and Sarah. It fosters an environment where those who are insensitive become sensitive. By acknowledging that a majority of our current members are very similar to the majority of those whom we wish to attract, leadership can craft a language that encourages sensitivity to others, a sensitivity that enriches our lives. A language of inclusion begins with the cultivation of sensitivity toward others.

Failure to turn off a cell phone while attending synagogue services is considered an act of insensitivity. Most people know that when they attend a lecture, concert, or a film, their phone needs to be turned off or, at the very least, put on silent vibrate mode. But people often forget, perhaps because cell phones have become such an integral part of daily life today. So they need to be reminded in a nonjudgmental way.

But how do we tell those who enter the synagogue on Shabbat to turn off their cell phones? Is there a better way than placing signs on the wall that read "Don't use the phone on Shabbat!" or "Turn off your cell phone!"? The answer is yes. We can convey the same message in language that shows an understanding of human nature, in this case the widespread tendency of people to forget to silence their cell phones. This shows sensitivity and is nonthreatening. In short, it's more reader-friendly. Instead of signs that make demands on people, we can post signs that say "Cell phone–free area" or "Enhance the mood: Put it on vibrate."

BUILDING WORDS OF WELCOME

The language with which an organization or synagogue characterizes itself gives people reasons to support, volunteer, and join. The initial language should be created by a committee of at least one senior professional and one senior volunteer. They need to come up with a series of phrases and statements that describe the importance of the organization. These phrases should be tested on staff and volunteers to see if they can be easily assimilated into normal conversation. If, after a few weeks of usage, they begin to be employed by others, then you know you are on the right track. The language needs to be supportive, welcoming, and inspiring, and it should be sufficiently specific to clearly reflect the mission of the organization or congregation.

BRANDING

The touchstone words and phrases chosen to describe the environment you hope to create often need to be movement-sensitive. Synagogues should seriously consider whether to include a movement label, such as Reform, Conservative/Masorti, or Reconstructionist, with the understanding that defining adjectives, adverbs, or additional phrasing will be required. Because synagogues reflect inner diversity, it's a disservice to simply brand yours as a Union of Reform Judaism (URJ) or United Synagogue of Conservative Judaism (USCJ) congregation. As much as those affiliations identify your synagogue in people's minds, you still have to add additional descriptive language.

For example, many synagogues describe themselves as "Conservative egalitarian" or "Modern Orthodox." A more effective brand might be "the comfortable shul," "a nurturing community," "a learning community," or "a community that studies the past to enhance meaning in the present," followed by its affiliation, if it has one, to a synagogue umbrella group, such as URJ and USCJ.

> A language of inclusion must foster an environment where those who are insensitive become sensitive. A language of inclusion begins with the cultivation of sensitivity toward others.

Creating a language of inclusion begins with key people asking the following questions and developing a series of suggested responses:

1. What does our name mean?
2. What do we stand for?
3. What will this organization offer me?
4. Does a language of inclusion include non-Jews?

These are questions of engagement. They help define who we are. Engagement in this exercise challenges committee and/or staff members to use words like "ethical," "committed," "authentic," "meaningful," "traditional," "halachic," and "Zionist," and results in the development of a vision that describes the desired nature of the community or organization.

My experience visiting synagogues and observing how Jewish organizations operate over the past three decades has taught me that Jewish leadership, both lay and professional, possess superb skills and are engaged in creative and meaningful work. But we are challenged by demographics. We see many of our institutions shrinking. We tend to believe that if we only modified our vision, we might attract new blood. That's only partially true. It's not just about changing demographics or reaching out by offering something for everyone. It's also about understanding, appreciating, and cultivating an inclusive volunteer culture. We need to do this more effectively. It begins with language, a particular language—a language of inclusion.

Talking Points

- How would you describe your organization's or synagogue's specific reputation in the community?

- Does the leadership of your organization speak with one voice, sending a consistent message about your organization's mission and culture? If so, how was this unified message crafted? If not, how would you go about forging a common language for your organization?

- What are three examples of inclusionary language used by the leadership of your organization?

- What are three examples of exclusionary language used by your organization's leadership?

- What steps could your organization take to improve the "welcoming" feeling of your organization's common language?

3

CULTIVATING VOLUNTEERS
Understanding Basic Myths

"*People just don't come forward to volunteer the way they used to.*"

"*Young parents don't have the time anymore. Both partners work and any leisure time they have is spent with their children.*"

"*Everyone wants to be on the fast track. If they can't serve on the board immediately, they don't want to give you the time.*"

These statements reflect the most common complaints heard in volunteer organizations. Yet, as with most complaints, they reflect only partial truths.

There is an art to cultivating volunteers. Some people can do it almost magically. Filled with an abundance of charisma, they attract volunteers like moths to a flame, for better or worse. And then there are the rest of us. No matter how hard we try, at least at first, we obtain only minimal results. Cultivating volunteers is hard work and it requires more than charisma. Volunteers can be attracted and successfully nurtured if you follow certain basic guidelines. Nurturing volunteers is an acquired skill.

After being a member of a synagogue for a number of years, I was approached by a member of the board. "Don't you work in the not-for-profit sector?"

"Yes I do," I replied.

"What exactly do you do?" asked the board member.

"I teach people how to build membership organizations."

"Wow, I know you must be very busy, but do you think we could have breakfast sometime? I'll invite another board member. We could really use your input."

"I'm sure I could find time. Just give me a call."

Two weeks later the board member, the synagogue president, and I met for breakfast. The lay leaders presented a situation to me, and I responded with advice. The volunteers took notes, and at the end of the meeting one of them said, "Thank you for agreeing to meet with us. You've certainly given us a lot to think about and to work with. We know that your professional life is extremely demanding and that you travel extensively. However, if you don't mind, we are going to add your name to the membership committee. When the committee meets, they mail a postcard that indicates the meeting's time and place. If you happen to be around and would like to attend, please do."

> People who view things in a negative light will always have a difficult time attracting volunteers. Attracting volunteers—and cultivating them—calls for positive thinking and positive actions.

Two weeks later I received a postcard in the mail, announcing the next membership committee meeting. As it happened, I was free that evening and decided to attend. Two months later, I was chairing the committee.

THE MYTHS
OF CULTIVATING VOLUNTEERS

The preceding scenario reflects a successful interaction that most likely would not have occurred with anyone who made the negative statements noted at the outset of this chapter. Why? Because people who view things in a negative light will always have a difficult time attracting volunteers. Attracting volunteers—and cultivating them—calls for positive thinking and positive actions. Let's address these myths one by one.

Debunking Myth 1

People just don't come forward to volunteer the way they used to. It's doubtful that hordes of volunteers have ever come forward, except perhaps during wartime. Even if larger numbers of people came forward fifty-plus years ago to help build synagogues and Jewish community institutions, it was a result of the move to suburbia, coupled with the need for community and the desire to retain Jewish identification in a new environment. Today's generations of Jews are comfortable in the secular world and have less of a need to build and support Jewish institutions—synagogues, JCCs, and schools. People might not come forward the way they used to, but they might come forward if they were approached properly.

There is an art to cultivating volunteers. Some people can do it almost magically. Filled with an abundance of charisma, they attract volunteers like moths to a flame, for better or worse. And then there are the rest of us.

Debunking Myth 2

Young parents don't have the time anymore. Both partners are working and any leisure time they have is spent with the children. It's true that life is more complicated and busier now than it was twenty, thirty, or forty years ago; however, forty years ago life was not simple, either. People will come forward if they sense a need, feel that they are needed, and are treated in a dignified and respectful manner.

Debunking Myth 3

Everyone wants to be on the fast track. If they can't serve on the board immediately, they won't give you the time. This statement reflects the view that a board appointment is the most prestigious and people will only volunteer when they are placed in positions of prominence. It is a fallacious assumption, and one that often indicates a personal bias. The truth is more complicated. More women are assuming positions of serious responsibility today, while it is becoming tougher to engage men. Both men and women, if properly asked and motivated, will become involved if their involvement gives them a challenge or a satisfying experience.

THE SUCCESSFUL APPROACH: STEP BY STEP

Let's analyze the successful scenario described earlier to figure out why it turned out so well.

1. The board member targeted the potential volunteer—me—and approached me by requesting advice. At the same time, the two people who met with me allayed my fears of being sucked into a volunteer position by prefacing the invitation with an acknowledgment of my busy schedule.

2. The board member followed up, arranging a meeting at the prospective volunteer's convenience. He brought the president of the organization with him, and the president took notes during the meeting. (I, the volunteer, was flattered and impressed by the sincerity of the organization's leadership. I was also impressed that the president thought this meeting was sufficiently important to attend.)

3. The board member and president thanked me, the targeted person.

4. The board member placed the targeted volunteer on a committee in a nonpressured manner.

Each of these actions is important, but the most vital one of all was that I was "asked" to participate and then "thanked" for my time. People like to be asked. People like to feel needed. It doesn't matter if volunteers are serving as ushers, cooks, envelope stuffers, fundraisers, or innovators; they all need to feel that their position is valued and that they are appreciated.

It doesn't matter if volunteers are serving as ushers, cooks, envelope stuffers, fundraisers, or innovators; they all need to feel that their position is valued and that they are appreciated.

When attracting volunteers, you must recognize that not everyone wants to be a committee chair or sit on a board. I have often observed volunteers who hold high-powered positions in the workplace spending an evening eating pizza and stuffing envelopes. Clearly, they did not step forward for the food or the challenge. They volunteered because they enjoy the social interaction and were made to feel that the few hours they donated were spent productively.

THANK YOU—I REALLY MEAN IT!

Volunteers need to be nurtured, just as they need to be asked, acknowledged, thanked, and motivated to get and stay involved. Leadership (professional or volunteer) must ensure that the time volunteers devote to a cause is a positive experience. This goes beyond simply expressing appreciation. A leader wishing to successfully involve volunteers has to make an initial judgment about their skills and abilities and then initiate a long-term strategy that will nurture and empower those volunteers over a protracted period.

Cultivating volunteers begins by acknowledging the prospective volunteer's gift of time. The simple act of thanking people for attending a meeting, even if it is assumed that they will attend, creates an opportunity for engagement.

In 2008, the vice chancellor of a major academic Jewish institution attended a dinner in my honor. It was a testimonial dinner, the eleventh plague of the not-for-profit world. By the time my speech rolled around, everyone was tired and the hour was late. I walked to the podium and immediately thanked everyone not for coming, but for staying. Six months later, at another meeting, the vice chancellor approached me and told me that my simple comment made the remainder of the evening bearable.

I attend twenty to thirty meetings with lay groups each year. I always begin by thanking them for attending. These people need to be thanked. They are giving us their time. I am humbled by the nature of their gift.

THE RIGHT WAY TO ASK

The second act in engaging a volunteer is the asking. People like to and need to be asked to help. Too often leadership or organizations simply assume that people will come forward, and are surprised when they don't. The failure of leadership to think through the volunteer engagement process often results in lost opportunities. Some people actually fill out questionnaires and mail them back, indicating that they would like to serve on a committee. When the congregation or organization fails to respond, those people will never offer their services again.

Volunteers need to be successful. So a leader who asks someone to accept a position has to provide sufficient support and information to ensure that the volunteer experience is a successful one.

SHOWING THE WAY

I remember a senior rabbi in a New England congregation who asked a congregant to accept a volunteer position as an usher for a forthcoming holiday. The volunteer tentatively accepted. The rabbi then personally escorted her to the office, introduced her to each member of the support staff, and explained how each of these people would be available to assist her. The volunteer left the synagogue feeling that she had sufficient support to do her job well.

That volunteer rose to a position of prominence in the synagogue after just three years. After each volunteer activity, she was thanked both privately and publicly. Within a few weeks after each time she volunteered, she was asked anew to assume another responsibility. Once she was asked to train a new volunteer to take her place. On another occasion she was asked to work on a small committee with a specific, well-defined goal. Step by step, she became more enamored of the synagogue and its community. Step by step, she was integrated into the synagogue committee and leadership structure.

Leaders—people in positions of authority—must understand that it is their responsibility to make people feel needed and appreciated—not just because of the tasks they are performing for the organization, but because you, as the leader, personally appreciate and value their time. Leaders need to display their interest in their volunteers and take the time to learn who they are as people. A leader who embodies these simple maxims will build loyalty and commitment in the volunteer pool.

CREATING OPPORTUNITIES FOR ENGAGEMENT

Once, a long time ago, I was serving as the rabbi in a small congregation, most of whose members were not ritually observant. Only a small percentage kept kosher homes. An equally small number attended Shabbat services regularly. The congregation's president had a mission: He wanted to see more people in synagogue on Shabbat. For most of these people, Judaism was more about identity than religion, a way to preserve their heritage and culture. For them, Friday evening services were more of a social gathering than a venue for worship. They viewed service attendance on Shabbat morning as a responsibility to grudgingly fulfill from time to time. The president asked me if there was anything I could do. How could I say no? We were both interested in the same thing. I thought about it for a while and then decided that something needed to be done to make people want to come to services.

The president and I agreed that I would explain to the congregation that because the building was in such dire need of repair, there was concern that a fire might break out. I explained this to the congregation on Yom Kippur, the holiest day of the year, and went on to say that, as a result of my fears, I had decided that the Torahs could no longer remain in the synagogue during the week until these concerns were addressed.

In the interim, I said, we were requesting that every family share the responsibility of caring for the Torahs in their home. We created a schedule that began with the Torahs being picked up after Shabbat had ended and then moving from house to house each night, where they would be hosted until the following Friday evening, when they would be returned to the synagogue. I informed the community that a list had been compiled, indicating who would be responsible for hosting each Torah, and the dates they would be responsible for the holy scroll.

> Leaders must understand that it is their responsibility to make people feel needed and appreciated—not just because of the tasks they are performing for the organization, but because you, as the leader, personally appreciate and value their time.

The congregation was stunned. They didn't know how to respond. I explained that they could understand this in one of two ways—mystically or practically. The mystical understanding was that the Torahs traveling from house to house from Shabbat to Shabbat paralleled the feminine aspect of God, the *Shechinah*, traveling in exile all week until she was reunited with the masculine counterpart of God. The practical understanding asked people to consider this as kind of a Torah time-sharing arrangement.

At the end of the prayer service, I removed one of the Torahs from the ark. The congregation's president removed the other. I carried mine into the middle of the sanctuary and presented it to a couple I'll call Dave and Mary. The other Torah was placed into the hands of another couple, Al and Ruby. I told each couple in front of the entire congregation that they had the responsibility to care for their Torah until the following evening, and then they needed to deliver it to the next two couples.

The Torahs visiting and living in members' homes changed the way the community functioned. Initially, people felt awkward and didn't know how to behave. Each family needed to think about covering their heads before they lifted it or, in some cases, entered the room where the Torah had been placed. Most people didn't know where to put it. It forced them to talk about the Torah. "Harry, can we leave it on the couch in the living room?" "Not if we are going to have people over."

"We couldn't put it on a shelf in the bathroom?"

"No, that would be really inappropriate."

"Nor on the kitchen table. Certainly not in our bedroom— I'm not getting undressed in front of a Torah!"

"The garage is too dirty."

Slowly but surely, everyone worked it out. Sometimes people would invite neighbors to come over for a viewing. "Rabbi, can I show the Torah to my non-Jewish neighbor?"

> What is the message we are attempting to deliver, and how will it be received? If we fail to ask and think through these questions, we may end up discouraging volunteers.

People tried to read from it. Some started wearing head coverings when they entered the house where the Torah currently resided. Others started saying blessings before they ate. Every Shabbat morning the hosts of the previous week were invited to shul for a special *aliyah* and blessing and were asked, as they stood with their hands on the Torah, what it was like to be a Torah host. It was a great experience. People started to attend services in the synagogue on a more regular basis.

OK, the impetus for this exercise was slightly contrived— on Yom Kippur, no less. But it was a powerful experience for everyone involved. I was very proud of what had been accomplished. For a short time, a lot of people were actively motivated and provided with a meaningful, enriching experience.

The experience of the traveling Torahs did more than just sensitize people and bring them to synagogue. It gave them the opportunity to feel like part of the community. They felt that they had accomplished something. It encouraged them to come forward as volunteers in other areas. People were brought together as a result of this shared experience and new friendships were formed; as a result, overall volunteer activity increased.

TURNED OFF OR BURNT OUT?

Volunteer turnoff is different from volunteer burnout and occurs much more frequently. Volunteer burnout happens over considerable time. Volunteer turnoff can happen relatively quickly. It looks like this: A volunteer assumes a position of responsibility, devotes a great deal of effort to succeeding, and then vanishes.

Too often this stems directly from the way the organizational structure and leadership interacted with that volunteer. Say a volunteer is charged with a responsibility or a committee portfolio, but she is not provided with a clear understanding of the chain of command, the organization's culture, or the limits of her authority. As a result, she finds herself undermined, misdirected, and encountering a host of unnecessary obstacles. If the experience is demoralizing, she finishes the required task and fades into the woodwork. Ouch!

Leaders need to ask themselves: What is the message we are attempting to deliver, and how will it be received? If we fail to ask and think through these questions, we may end up discouraging volunteers. Consider the numerous times people have been appointed to committees and never been properly briefed on their responsibility as a committee member. Consider the message that a volunteer gets when he is given a committee appointment or a position with no formal guidance.

While it might not be the case, the message that is delivered is that the board's request was not sincere. It was simply a matter of lip service. The real message was: "Volunteers not welcome. Don't bother applying!"

How *Not* to Handle a Volunteer

Bob, an executive in an international legal firm, was asked to be the fundraising chair for his child's private school. He was told that the school needed to raise $100,000 more to meet a projected deficit. Bob went to work immediately: He formed a committee, decided on an event, set a date and a price. He called the school development office and provided them with a list of tasks he wanted them to complete by a given date.

The development office was understaffed and already overloaded with work. The head of development called the school president, who told Bob that he couldn't use school staff. Bob was disappointed but not deterred. Committed to running a successful event, he engaged a person to assist him at his own expense and proceeded with the planning. He decided that the event highlight would be a dialogue between several Nobel Prize winners. He began selling tickets. Since Bob's firm represented the Nobel Peace Prize committee, he was confident that he could enlist some of the prize winners for support.

Bob called the school president, shared his ideas, and obtained permission to move forward. One of Bob's strategies was to solicit the board members for a private party with the prize winners. He was confident that the party would raise most of the funds needed, allowing him to sell the remaining tickets at a nominal cost. Bob was sure that this event would be successful.

That's when the president told Bob he did not like the idea of a private party and that Bob would have to raise the funds another way. Bob canceled the event and resigned.

What did Bob do wrong? Had he failed to understand the limits of his responsibilities? Had he overstepped his authority? Did he really have any authority? What happened here?

Bob was accustomed to working on his own and assumed that as committee chair he had full authority. Would he have been more successful if the school had provided him with appropriate guidelines when he accepted the responsibility as fundraising chair? Should he have been told that he needed to provide a complete plan before proceeding, and that it needed to be cleared by the school president?

Note that Bob's decisions were countermanded at each step of the process. Had a clear line of command been established at the outset, he might still be raising funds for his child's school. Instead, Bob continuously felt undermined and second-guessed. Rather than encouraging Bob's volunteer activities and tapping into his considerable enthusiasm for the task he had accepted, the school discouraged him and left him with a sour taste. Presto! Volunteer turnoff!

Bottom line: Bob did everything right and should have been nurtured and encouraged every step of the way. The school culture failed to understand how to work with volunteers. School leadership should have been more sensitive to him and taken a long-range view of Bob and his abilities. They should have understood that if Bob had been properly nurtured, he could have been cultivated to serve on the board and help the school for years to come. If the school leadership had been supportive instead of resistant, Bob would be thanking them for allowing him to raise funds for the school.

Cultivating volunteers is a serious business. Just as a not-for-profit organization must focus on its budget and fiscal activities, so, too, does it need to devote time and effort toward creating an atmosphere that will attract and nurture volunteers.

Talking Points

• What will motivate potential volunteers to sign on to your organization?

• What positive actions do members of your organization take to attract and cultivate volunteers?

• Describe your three most involved volunteers. What roles do they play in your organization? How have their roles changed since they first signed on?

• What makes for a satisfying volunteer experience in your organization?

• How can you help your existing volunteers or potential volunteers feel more appreciated?

• What policies does your organization have in place to help leaders recognize and honor volunteer contributions?

4

THE BOARD
OF DIRECTORS

Is the Herring Rotten
in the Head?

I remember the first time I attended a synagogue board meeting. As a newly ordained rabbi, I dressed for the occasion. I was finally going to see the leaders of my community, magnates of industry, wrestle with the many issues that confront a synagogue. I was twenty-seven years old, had never attended a board meeting, and was filled with excitement. I couldn't have been more disappointed.

The evening service was about to begin in the chapel. But board members entering the synagogue ignored the service and the requests to attend. Some of them actually waved to us. Had they no shame? They marched up the stairs to the board room, soldiers poised to do battle. They entered the library. The chairs were arranged in rows, classroom style. The board members took their seats in what appeared to be a predetermined order. The president sat at a desk facing them.

This is what I had been waiting for. I had spent seven years at the seminary preparing to lead a community as a rabbi. While I was only the assistant rabbi, I knew that someday that would change. Someday I would have my own synagogue. I looked for my senior colleague. He was standing at the other side of the room, whispering something to one of the officers. He didn't have a seat next to the president.

"Where does the rabbi sit?" I asked a board member sitting near me. "Oh, usually in the corner. He isn't ordinarily permitted to stay for the entire meeting. We made an exception this evening when we invited you to deliver the lesson of the week."

I couldn't believe it. Was it possible that the rabbi was not the CEO? How was it possible that the rabbi was not permitted to attend a board meeting? I remembered my instructor telling us in class last year that it was absolutely necessary for the rabbi to attend all board meetings!

The president called for reports to be read. Budget and finance took an hour. Ritual took thirty minutes, as the chair assured all present that the defenders of the faith were not interested in permitting a group of young families to introduce more experiential liturgy. A discussion followed as to whether or not the synagogue would remain affiliated with its parent movement. "It's too costly for what we are receiving," said one board member.

Following that, the vote to disaffiliate was tabled for a future meeting. The cemetery committee reported that people continued to die and that was a profit center for the synagogue.

Finally, the chair of the youth committee was called on for a report. She requested that additional funds be allocated to engage a better qualified youth director for the teens. The treasurer informed her that the requested funds weren't in the budget. That's when the yelling started. "How can we spend $25,000 on a piece of decorative sculpture and not have $5,000 to invest in our children's future?!"

Three hours later I returned home. I was exhausted. I had witnessed grown adults raising their voices and unnecessarily interrupting one another. I had seen people with means abusing their authority, and I had listened to lengthy, eloquent speeches devoid of any substance but clearly satisfying the speaker—all in the name of religion!

I had been baptized.

The not-for-profit world is filled with boards that attract and cultivate serious people with vision and that are governed in a well-executed manner. Unfortunately, a number of not-for-profit organizations are led by people who, in many instances, lack the necessary skills to attract serious leadership and to govern wisely.

During the time that I spent in my first congregation, I came to appreciate the depth of commitment of many of the people who served on the board. I also came to realize that serving on a board didn't guarantee serious commitment, nor did it guarantee productivity or prevent people from posturing.

People are appointed to serve on boards for a number of different reasons, and people choose to serve on boards for a variety of reasons as well. This chapter was written for the institutions with boards that need help.

In the past thirty-five years, I have attended all kinds of board meetings: camp boards, synagogue boards, Holocaust organization boards; boards of JCCs, afternoon religious schools, and day schools. Some functioned in an effective and serious manner. Others did not.

BOARDS ARE COMPLICATED

The role of the board of directors in a not-for-profit institution is extremely complicated. Even though basic aims and goals are often written into their charters, the practical planning, thinking, and envisioning of what it takes to maintain a healthy, thriving institution are not. People bring to a board a host of skills and an equal number of challenges. It is the task of the professional and senior volunteer leadership to guide the board to address issues of organizational concern.

In addition to being managers, professionals face continuous challenges. They need to attract volunteers and members and, when necessary, engage them actively. Concurrently, they need to target and nurture an additional group of volunteers, a "farm team," who have the ability to eventually assume positions of leadership. Perhaps because these pressures are so numerous, and volunteer and professional leadership have such limited time, the task of identifying, cultivating, and training volunteers and future leaders often falls by the wayside.

> Because these pressures are so numerous, and volunteer and professional leadership have such limited time, the task of identifying, cultivating, and training volunteers and future leaders often falls by the wayside.

A successful organization values and nurtures board growth and development. Too often, an organization fails to understand that board orientation and training need to be integral to its culture.

In order for an organization to thrive, it must target, select, motivate, and train prospective board members in a well-conceived effort that identifies specific people for committees and others for the board. Oftentimes, small- to medium-sized organizations designate board members to chair committees. This is not an ideal situation, because an effective board needs to be trained to view committee recommendations from a policy point of view, and a committee chair may lose that perspective as ownership of the committee's "turf" colors her thought process.

IT STARTS AT THE TOP

There is an old Yiddish proverb: The herring is rotten in the head. It means that the problem starts at the top. If only it were so simple! Organizational strength is more than a by-product of its current leadership; it is a result of an ongoing thought process that has usually been in place for a number of years and is reinforced by the organization's culture. To strengthen an existing synagogue or not-for-profit, leadership must begin by understanding the components that are part of its culture. Consider the following cautionary tale as indicative of less than positive cultures.

Two gentlemen meet before a synagogue board meeting. They have not seen each other for nearly a year. One says to the other, "So how've you been?"

The other replies, "I've been."

"Anything exciting on tonight's agenda?"

"I hope not. I only attend these meetings to restore my sense of normalcy."

"Normalcy?"

"Yes, no matter how the world changes, the arguments and discussions always remain the same."

"I know. All we discuss is money."

"Decisions have already been made by the time we get to the meeting. I feel abused."

"That's exactly it. All they want is my money—never my advice."

Serving on a board of directors can be a stimulating activity that motivates and inspires people to take that extra step to increase their volunteer commitment. A successful board meeting can reinforce the organization's mission and leave its members convinced that their actions and support make a difference. Yet how many people leave board meetings frustrated or angry when they should feel the satisfaction of a job well done? How many people view their service as an obligation instead of an opportunity for inspiration? A successful board meeting entails more than just passing a budget or pushing through someone's agenda. For a board meeting to be considered a success, board members need to walk out with a sense of accomplishment and progress.

ABUSED AND MISUNDERSTOOD

The board of directors is perhaps the most misunderstood group in the not-for-profit world. Theoretically, these boards are the policymaking body for their organization; at the same time, the people who serve on these boards are those who most need to be motivated. They are the rainmakers, and yet the manner in which board members are treated and prepared for their position rarely reflects the time and support they give to the board enterprise. It doesn't matter whether an organization is locally based or international: Board members donate considerable time and talent to the organization—most likely money, too. So transforming a negative or neutral board meeting into one that is positive and energizing begins with the realization that planning board meetings requires serious thought and an appropriate amount of staff and volunteer time.

If we attempt to calculate the amount of staff and volunteer time that went into the planning and execution of an effective board meeting and add to it an hourly fee to cover the time of each board member, we would quickly realize that the costs we are talking about are significant. Members of the board deserve an experience that is equal to the cost and time involved. Board meetings need to be viewed as more than a forum for reporting to a group of people whose financial support is needed. More often than not, staff and decision-making leadership think of the board as peripheral—a rubber stamp for decisions already made beforehand. They fail to recognize that the people attending the board meeting represent the organization's current leadership. It would be doing the institution a disservice not to maximize these opportunities.

> A successful board meeting entails more than just passing a budget or pushing through someone's agenda. Board members need to walk out with a sense of accomplishment and progress.

Serving on a board is an honor, and needs to be perceived by board members and the community at large in that light. To retain existing board members and to attract potential new board members, people need to be treated with dignity and empowered with a sense of mission. Board training and orientation, if seriously instituted and integrated into the organizational culture, will create a firm groundwork for future leadership.

DEVELOPING AN EFFECTIVE BOARD

To forge an effective board, a well-developed plan that weaves lay training into the culture of the organization so it successfully attracts and nurtures the appropriate people is needed. A well-chosen board member should strengthen the organization's ability to fulfill its mission and create an ambassador of the organization's culture. Unfortunately, some boards fail to conceptualize the nature of this role before they begin the recruitment process.

Integrating New Board Members

Volunteer organizations rarely consider how to integrate new board members into the organizational culture. International organizations and academic institutions, as well as locally based organizations, need to make new board members feel proud and valued. On several occasions, I have witnessed the process that a number of academic institutions employ to introduce new members to the board. Instead of creating an opportunity for the new board member to become engaged, a simple biography and welcome seemed to suffice. After that it was business as usual. This method often results in serious, high-powered people feeling like ducks out of water, a distinctly uncomfortable feeling. A more effective strategy would entail inviting new board members to meet with a small group of people in a relaxed, social setting before the meeting and assigning each new member a "buddy." This approach would create an atmosphere of warmth and forge a strong sense of allegiance to the organization.

> A well-chosen board member should strengthen the organization's ability to fulfill its mission and create an ambassador of the organization's culture.

I'M IN CHARGE, I'M ON THE BOARD

People are attracted to boards for a variety of reasons. Many are disappointed once they begin to serve because they have not been properly clued in to the organization's culture. Some board members will view their appointment to a not-for-profit board as if it were an appointment to the board of a multinational corporation. These people have never served—and most likely will never serve—on the board of a multinational corporation. As a result, they might act or view their new status in a way that is more reflective of their fantasy about the position than the reality of the organization's culture. This type of thinking can cause all kinds of difficulties with staff and within the organization itself.

Rebecca was just elected to a board of her synagogue. In addition she was given a portfolio of membership acquisition. She immediately called the office and asked the staff to send her all kinds of information. It was a logical request, but the synagogue staff had previously scheduled mailings and a host of other tasks that took priority.

"But I'm on the board," Rebecca told the office manager. "I need this information now!"

It was a simple request, but one that the small office staff simply was not in a position to fulfill, at least for a while. Rebecca was frustrated and angry. She should have been informed by a senior board member of what to reasonably expect from the staff.

Sometimes those who seek to serve on a board are satisfied with holding the position and view their role on the board merely as a position of status. This can result in a nonproductive board member, the curse of a not-for-profit organization, especially if the board's main purpose is to raise funds.

Finally, there are those who serve on boards who recognize that the experience will involve all types of people with various agendas. They understand that at times it will be frustrating and at times it will be productive, and in spite of it all, it will satisfy their desire to be a successful volunteer.

Conversely, a number of organizations specifically select people in the community with status and the ability to make substantial financial contributions to serve on their boards. This approach may have merit in certain circumstances, but additional criteria should be required. Board members who feel they have been selected solely because they have the means will rarely become effective leaders and champions of the cause unless they have been sufficiently motivated and empowered.

ESTABLISH NEEDS TO MEET NEEDS

It is not uncommon for boards to select and ultimately elect new members without first determining the qualities the organization needs in its board members. Rather than developing a plan and then searching for specific people to put that plan into action, organizations often choose to accept anyone who comes forward. A number of national and international volunteer organizations simply ask their branches or regions to nominate people for board positions and hope the people have the talents the board needs.

This strategy rarely yields a strong board. For one thing, it projects an image to the community at large that the board lacks focus and organization. This, in turn tends to discourage high caliber candidates from coming forward in the future. By contrast, boards that call for volunteers with specific skills show prospective board members that they have thought through the process and have tapped these individuals because they have something valuable to contribute.

Local organizations can often exercise more discretion in board selection. Unfortunately, many of them will commit the same errors in judgment, appointing people to serve in positions just because they have expressed an interest or because volunteers are difficult to find, rather than waiting, searching, and selecting the proper person.

ORIENTATION OR ALIENATION?

A number of chambers of commerce and national Jewish organizations have instituted three-hour board orientation programs for prospective board members before they are formally installed. The orientation session is devoted to explaining the role board members are expected to play. Most not-for-profit organizations prepare orientation packets for a potential or future board member. This reflects good intentions but usually produces minimal results. Some organizations actually fail to specify what is expected of a member of the board of directors, setting new board members up for failure. Orientation sessions are a worthy introduction to an organization's culture; however, they need to be viewed as the first step in a long-range plan designed to raise the overall level of board commitment. The cultivation of board members is an extension of the same plan designed to attract and involve volunteers. Board orientation also requires follow-up. Volunteer leadership or staff should plan training programs ahead of time, and appropriate follow-up should be scheduled as well. Then, those who conducted the orientation and training should return to these congregations six months later to conduct interviews to ascertain if programs are effective and what changes are still necessary.

Most organizations are multidimensional. They are composed of committees, boards, and supporters. Consider how strong and vibrant an organization could be if committee members, board members, and supporters were united in a common culture and spoke in one voice. Contrast this imagined view with that of any functioning organization you are familiar with. Is the organization you envision bound by a common cause on the committee, board, and outside supporter level? Do each of these strands (committee, board, and supporters) articulate the same vision? Do the organization's leaders model personal behavior that dovetails with the organization's culture and spreads across the dimensions?

Some organizations are built on a foundation of distrust and dissent. Such a culture could attract people with high ideals; however, the manner in which the organization conducts itself may dissuade people of vision from making a long-term commitment. It may also attract people whose personal ambitions may deter and prevent their understanding of how a healthy organization should operate and whose narrow focus may override the greater organizational vision. An unhealthy culture usually spawns weak, ineffectual leaders. Sometimes the job makes the person. One would hope that the person makes the job.

Oftentimes, local organizations appoint people to board positions without providing them with clear expectations. This can result in people who have intended to serve as funders being asked to engage in activities other than those they thought they were signing on for, or workers being placed in positions other than those that are task-oriented. Establishing clear expectations is crucial when appointments are made.

Too often, especially when it comes to boards of large organizations with regional, national, or international missions, leaders utilize board meetings for "show and tell," to discuss day-to-day operations or to explain programmatic initiatives that are taking place, rather than calling on the board for policy-making and organization building. These approaches make for a passive board and hinder that board from developing into an active one. Diverting a board's attention and making it function like a committee undermine the integrity of the organization. Distracting board members from their core policymaking role creates an impediment to future board development.

The Federation of Jewish Men's Clubs reinvents itself every two to three years. This began in 2003 when the group adopted a strategic plan. The plan called for the elimination of committee work when the board met. Items that required discussion were allotted appropriate time. This wasn't an easy change to implement. It began with an orientation and discussion about how volunteer time needed to be respected. This included a discussion about officer, board, and committee chairs' expectations. One of the outcomes of these discussions was an understanding that in order for everyone's time to be respected, it was crucial for all committee reports to be read before meetings; discussions would only focus on questions raised by committee chairs. Nearly a year had to pass before FJMC leadership was able to adapt to this new way of thinking. As a result of these changes, meetings and discussions that used to take two to three days are completed in half the time, and additional opportunities for discussions about the future of the FJMC have become available.

I once attended a board meeting in a synagogue in North Carolina. The board was provided with a regular report on the status of its efforts to target, recruit, and engage new members. The board also listened to a plan to socially integrate the incoming board of directors. The board member in charge of new board orientation developed in committee a handbook explaining how this would assist the synagogue and how the board needed to learn to respond. This is an excellent way of helping a board to focus.

Not too many years ago, a new Jewish private school was created in Manhattan. It was organized by a group of would-be parents and some acquaintances of means who believed a new school with a specific philosophy was needed. The school's founders deliberately constructed the board to ensure that philanthropists, parents, and educators would all be represented. At the time, this blend "felt right." However, over time it evolved into a board where all members appeared to be equal but some were more equal than others. The parents and educators often lacked the financial and, in some instances, the social sophistication to assume leadership positions. Invariably, their issues were not issues that needed to be brought before a board and would have been better dealt with by committees.

BOARD OR COMMITTEE?
WHERE DO I BELONG?

People chosen for a board must be selected because of their talents and acumen, and those talents must be appropriately engaged. Equally important, people who are selected to serve on committees must be targeted and chosen for similar reasons. Depending on the organization, the committee structure does not have to serve as the training ground for future board members. As organizations change—and change is a given for any organization—people with different qualities and skills need to be shifted to different positions. An organization that creates a healthy respect for people will be able to sort and re-sort appropriate people for committees and for positions on the board without ill effect.

FAST-TRACKING—A SIGN
OF ORGANIZATIONAL WEAKNESS

Ongoing recruitment is the lifeblood of an organization. Yet too often organizations attempt to recruit and involve new volunteers by placing them on a "fast track." I have seen this occur in synagogues, agencies, academic institutions, and community centers. Usually, it is a shortsighted effort that means the institution or organization is operating from a position of weakness. Organizations justify fast-tracking because they fear that if the volunteer is not offered a position of prominence, such as a board position, he will lose interest and become involved elsewhere. Fast-tracking often results in the volunteer's failure to learn about and become integrated into

> As organizations change—and change is a given for any organization—people with different qualities need to be shifted to different positions.

the organization's culture. Fast-tracking also may promote a sense of importance that is not justified by the member's knowledge and experience.

Rather than learning how an organization fulfills its mission, the person who is being fast-tracked ends up being asked to understand policy without having the experience of working and grasping the contours of the playing field. Rapid advancement through the organizational structure without an appropriate training and orientation period are also potentially divisive. They imply a weakness in the committee structure and reinforce the notion that committee work will not be inspiring or productive and that the committees themselves might be ineffectual.

A successful board makes successful committee appointments by recognizing that everyone who serves on a committee will not necessarily rise to the board level. Committee appointments need to be understood as part of an overarching strategy designed to involve and train volunteers. Committees are one of the testing grounds for success and should be treated with the importance they deserve.

Finally, people who have been fast-tracked rarely develop the organizational loyalty that organizations seek.

KEY TOOLS FOR KEY PEOPLE

There are a number of tools that organizations use to educate board members. The successful volunteer organization understands this as a normal outgrowth of its culture. By contrast, the unsuccessful organization usually institutes board education as an afterthought. To seriously engage an existing board of directors, leadership needs to ask: What do we want the board members to know? What do we need them to tell others? If organizational leadership cannot answer these questions in one sentence, they will not be able to institute an effective board training program, and the end product will be poorly educated and improperly motivated board members.

In order to increase board involvement, some organizations conduct one-time or annual board retreats. Board retreats bring together a group of people for a particular period and can, in the short term, unite the group in common purpose and create an initial sense of camaraderie. For such retreats to be successful, however, groundwork for achieving long-term goals must be established, and proper follow-up is essential.

Another way organizations attempt to sensitize and educate a board is through brief presentations during the course of a meeting; these are designed to more fully educate board members about the workings of a particular aspect of the institution. This kind of brief presentation can be a helpful educational tool, but it will only be effective in motivating board members if designated members are asked to investigate the activity further and share their reactions at the next meeting. In this way, a simple presentation can be transformed into an opportunity for further board involvement.

FORGIVING A UNITED FRONT

As leaders seek to stimulate board development, they must keep one salient point in mind: Leadership needs to be united in process. This is a simple statement, but it is too often misunderstood and neglected. Process begins with lay leadership gathering together key people before a board meeting and obtaining the consent of all assembled to reinforce at the meeting the organization's vision, the challenges being suggested, and the relationships being built. The process of involving current and incoming board members through the articulation of short- and long-term goals, coupled with the reinforcement of a vision that challenges people to want to succeed, makes all the difference.

Two of the most important tools in this process of projecting a unified front are "asking" and "establishing relationships."

People like to be asked for their opinions and need to be asked in order to motivate them to assume positions of responsibility. Those who accept a position on a board, regardless of the motivations that attracted them to this position in the first place, have expressed a willingness to become involved. It is the leadership's responsibility to determine how to transform that willingness into action.

The second tool is leadership's ability to establish personal relationships and convey a sense of concern about the person. A phone call from the president to a board member invariably has a substantial positive effect. Touching base, asking about someone's health, expressing congratulations on a child's wedding or sympathy when a loss occurs, thanking a person for participating—all are powerful acts that make impressions that are rarely forgotten. People appreciate it when others reach out to them. This simple strategy is too often overlooked.

> The process of involving current and incoming board members through the articulation of short- and long-term goals, coupled with the reinforcement of a vision that challenges people to want to succeed, makes all the difference.

Naysayers often claim that it is impossible to cultivate an engaged board of directors that is geographically dispersed in the absence of regional staff members. They also see it as nearly impossible to nurture a local board when people's time commitments are limited. In an age of instantaneous communication, however, board members can always be involved by taking advantage of technology to create dialogues, forums, and ongoing interaction. Well-structured conference calls offer an opportunity for current and future leaders to think, to motivate others, and to shine. The key is to develop a set of goals and view the board as the venue from which future leadership will emerge.

Lay and professional leaders must understand their boards as they currently are and strive to make them stronger, more vibrant, and more responsive to community needs—united by language to a vision that reflects the desired culture. Boards in the not-for-profit world need to be viewed as "works in process," with the end game being continued progress.

Talking Points

• How would you characterize your board's culture?

• How much time and what percentage of your budget does your organization devote to targeting and training future board members? Do you think this is sufficient? Why or why not?

• What motivates your committee and board members?

• How could you better prepare and train your board members for the challenges they face?

• Why are some of your board members dissatisfied with the organization? What could you do to alleviate that dissatisfaction and make them more engaged in your organization's mission?

5

HOW DO WE WORK TOGETHER?

The Volunteer-Staff Dynamic

Ideal staff can at times feel like committed volunteers. Sensitive volunteer leaders can help make this happen. However, the process of working toward that ideal state calls for a well-developed strategic plan. All staff members need to feel appreciated. How an organization chooses to demonstrate this appreciation varies, depending on the task and the organization's culture.

Proper staff motivation requires more than just a thank-you for a job well done. It requires more than the token gift of a briefcase or a service pin. It requires strategic thinking and the full support of top lay leaders who are in agreement that staff who feel appreciated will remain loyal and motivated.

If properly motivated, staff—both senior and subordinate—will demonstrate the same devotion to the cause as a dedicated volunteer. A volunteer board of directors that understands how to make this happen can turn paid "work" into "callings."

A number of years ago I was part of a team transformed by the vision of a lay leader. His name was Jules Porter. Jules was raised in Los Angeles, where he was literally taken off the streets and nurtured by Rabbi Hillel Silverman, then the spiritual leader of Sinai Temple in Los Angeles. Jules became active in his synagogue men's club, where he took a FJMC Hebrew class that changed his life by enabling him for the first time to fully participate in religious services. The experience motivated him to become increasingly active in the FJMC; when I met him, he was on the way to becoming FJMC international president.

Jules Porter had a dream. It was to create a series of how-to books that would encourage and teach Jews to participate in Jewish life, beginning with a book explaining the Friday evening Shabbat dinner ritual. He believed that cadres of volunteers could be taught, with the help of the book, to serve as instructors.

> Proper staff motivation requires more than just a thank-you for a job well done, a the token gift of a briefcase or service pin. It requires strategic thinking and the full support of top lay leaders.

I was initially skeptical. Nonetheless, Jules convinced the FJMC board to support him and he began soliciting donations to fund the effort. He also convinced me to go along for the ride. We traveled the length and breadth of the country, seeking donors to assist us in this work. We raised the funds, engaged Dr. Ron Wolfson, who was teaching at what was then called the University of Judaism in Los Angeles (now American Jewish University), and created the Art of Jewish Living series.

The series began with the book about the Shabbat dinner ritual and eventually expanded to include volumes about conducting a meaningful Passover Seder, comforting mourners, and the message of Hanukkah. The books were originally published by the Federation of Jewish Men's Clubs, but after a number of years Jewish Lights, the publisher of this book, took them over.

Over the course of the year that we developed the book series, Jules motivated me and convinced me and my staff that this project had the potential to change the nature of American

Jewish culture. It became our project as well as his project. It challenged FJMC leaders to become lay instructors and to model this initiative. It transformed the way our organization functioned.

SENIOR STAFF:
MOTIVATIONS AND LIMITATIONS

Lay leadership can galvanize staff, just as senior staff can impact lay leadership. But senior professional staff also need to recognize their limitations to avoid a number of problems.

In some cases, when volunteers meet as a board they morph from friends into lay leaders. Their priorities may change as they are forced to align their thinking with institutional needs. This can put them at odds with professionals, who may differ over priorities and solutions to problems. When this happens, it can be difficult for many professionals, congregational rabbis in particular, who may experience this change of focus as a betrayal of friendship.

At seminary I once took a course in what I'll label pulpit politics. My instructor said something that decades later I often remember and repeat as a warning to my own students:

"Never expect to be appreciated for the number of hours you put in or the number of new members who join because of you. As far as the board's concerned, that's your job and you're expected to succeed. Your successes won't translate into bargaining chips when you renegotiate your contract. They won't win you any adulation other than the temporary satisfaction you will feel for a job well done. Hopefully, your actions will result in a change in the way some people think and decide to live their lives. But if you think, even for a minute, that your board owes you thanks, you are in the wrong profession."

Rabbis may not like to be thought of as mere synagogue staff, but on one level that's all they are. They are expected to get results, as is any other employee. That's why they're being paid. My instructor's words, painful as they were to hear, were said to protect our class of future rabbis from the harsh reality of the life we would face in the congregational trenches.

But the fact remains that rabbis, just like any other employee, want to be acknowledged for their good work. Our sense of self-worth depends, at least in part, on the recognition we receive from others.

Failure to be appreciated is one of the major reasons Jewish clergy leave the profession. Some rabbis make the erroneous assumption that congregants owe them because they supported those congregants in a time of need; others brag that lay leadership will "do anything for me," seriously misreading synagogue life. The rabbi—or any not-for-profit professional, for that matter—who expects to share the lifestyle of major donors is unconsciously competing with them for status. These types of behavior have a deleterious impact on many professionals and set the stage for failure.

I am often telephoned by congregational presidents or rabbi search committee chairs asking my private opinion about a candidate. In addition to questions about a particular rabbi's qualifications, I often hear the following: "Rabbi, we know that Rabbi 'X' is also talking to other congregations. Do you have any suggestions that will encourage him or her to choose us?"

I respond with the following questions: "Have you considered anything you can offer a prospective rabbi that might tip the scales in your favor? Is there are anything you can do for your prospective new rabbi that will raise his or her estimation of your community?"

The usual response I receive is, "Like what?"

"Well," I continue, "once on the job, rabbis rarely have the time to visit other congregations to learn what they are doing. Why not tell your prospective rabbi that you think it is important for the rabbi to have the opportunity to find out what is occurring in other congregations and that you want your rabbi and his or her family to spend at least one weekend every eight months visiting another congregation at your expense? The expense is nominal, even if it involves airfare and hotel, and it sends a strong message that you care about your rabbi. You want your rabbi to learn. Think what your rabbi will tell his or her colleagues about your congregation. 'My congregation cares enough about me to encourage me to visit other congregations to learn what's going on.'" Or, I suggest, why not encourage the rabbi to take a few days off sometime after the High Holy Day period? You will be surprised how appreciative your rabbi will be as a result of your simple acknowledgment and suggestion. He or she will return from this brief respite renewed and feeling supported. Words cannot convey how much this does to build loyalty and strengthen the relationship between the rabbi and the institution.

> Staff appreciation is the first of the necessary steps toward staff embracing organizational beliefs and goals. Staff appreciation starts at the top.

I have witnessed major shifts in attitudes as a result of the reassurance and positive feedback that senior and support staff have received. Staff appreciation is the first of the necessary steps toward staff embracing organizational beliefs and goals. Staff appreciation starts at the top. Lay leadership and senior staff need to say things like "thank you" and "good job."

ENGAGING THE RANKS

Senior staff, such as rabbis, cantors, and educators, generally receive a great deal of attention in synagogues and organizations—after all, they are senior staff—but the support staff are equally important and cannot be neglected or ignored. If the first step toward building a strong staff commitment is emotional support, the second step is engagement. Engagement leads to ownership.

Robert, a new JCC CEO, was brought in to turn around a declining organization. The board was unhappy. Membership and fundraising were at an all-time low. Staff turnover was at an all-time high. At his initial staff meeting he asked, "What's wrong with this place?" He followed that with: "What are you doing, and what should you be doing?"

Robert brought the one-hour meeting to a close by thanking everyone and informing them he would respond to their comments shortly. The staff felt that, for the first time, someone was concerned about them. Their change of attitude was the first of many steps toward institutional transformation.

It is unfair to assume that staff know how to be supportive, helpful, and engaging in all situations. Support staff interact with board members, volunteers, and the public, including congregants in a synagogue and clients in a community organization. They encounter a host of different situations on a daily basis and are called on to respond to them in a personal and sensitive manner.

> It is unfair to assume that staff know how to be supportive, helpful, and engaging in all situations.

Support staff employed by a not-for-profit organization need to be reminded on a regular basis that they are in a "service fulfillment profession."

Volunteer organizations can be likened to the hospitality industry, and it can't hurt for staff to think of themselves as akin to employees at a major hotel. I have known several directors of not-for-profit organizations who have had their staffs trained by people in the hotel management field. The staff members are taught to respond to clients as workers do, which is to say with genuine graciousness and a desire to please above all else.

Service fulfillment professionals must learn how to respond to volunteers in a similar manner. They need to be taught that everyone with whom they interact is a client. Sometimes volunteers cross the line. Staffers may be offended, feel attacked, and respond in an equally inappropriate manner, only to later regret an action that most likely cannot be undone. Staff need to learn how not to engage when angry but instead to keep doing what they have been trained to do.

All staffers want to feel that their efforts make a difference. Successful lay leadership interacts well with staff. Both groups need to be included in the consultative and planning process if they are to form an effective team. Staff members who are not included will feel estranged, and that will be reflected in their work habits.

Sometimes staff members are viewed as overly "in charge," "rude," "difficult," or "lazy." This may be the case, but the perception may also result from the way lay leadership and senior staff have unconsciously been taught to think. Staff members who are consistently ignored and never asked for input will feel isolated, unimportant, and unmotivated; consequently, they will be viewed as lazy. Staff members who appear to be overly "in charge" or come across as "difficult" may feel that they are not being heard. If this is the case, then the effectiveness of the volunteer organization will be challenged, and the status of staff members should be reexamined.

Staff do not always function effectively even when strong working partnerships do exist. People still require supervision, and mistakes and incidents that show poor judgment can still occur. Staffers may adopt short-term views and in doing so fail to make the most of situations they encounter.

A number of years ago, I staffed a booth at a rabbinical convention to promote the second book in the Art of Jewish Living series, *The Passover Seder.* One of my colleagues approached me to purchase the book. I'll never forget his comment: "I used your Art of Jewish Living book, *The Shabbat Seder,* to teach a course. It was wonderful. I didn't have to prepare any further."

He had saved an hour's preparation. More than likely, he taught perhaps ten people in the class. If he had followed the instructions in the teacher's guide and spent that same hour training three laypeople to serve as instructors, he could have had thirty people involved and spent his time doing something more productive. Staffers (even rabbis) sometimes have a tendency to do what is easiest and often seek short-term solutions when long-term thinking would be more effective.

STAFF-BOARD COMMUNICATIONS

Staff-board perceptions and the manner in which positive working relationships are forged depend on key aspects of their interaction. Each element is critical to the establishment of strong working relationships. Staff-board relationships are not based solely on lines of authority. They are based on clear understandings of expectations and the chain of command, coupled with positive reinforcement. A strong working relationship begins with both staff and board members accepting that in order to maximize efficiency and minimize confusion, communication needs to flow through predesignated channels. Board members need to be sensitized and reminded that support and senior staff have responsibilities that must be met in a timely fashion. Similarly, staff need to be empowered to explain to a board member that a request will be addressed, but certain predetermined tasks take priority.

Linking the Chain of Command

Who are the faceless voices on the other end of the phone that speak with such authority?

Who are the people who wander into the office seemingly at random and make demands of me?

How should I respond? What if one of their demands conflicts with what I'm supposed to do?

How do I say no?

Those are the sort of questions staffers must consider when dealing with board members. Staff-board procedures need to be clearly spelled out so that they have ready answers. An unplanned visit to the office by a board member can result in staff confusion and an interruption of normal office work.

Steve, a local board member, has a habit of strolling into the JCC on his way to lunch meetings. He often brings candy and donuts for the staff. Everyone likes him. But last week he asked Dolores, one of the JCC secretaries, to find a hotel for a friend of his who would be coming to visit. Dolores didn't know what to do. She feared that saying "no" would offend him. However, if she agreed, she would have to rearrange her office priorities. How should she respond?

All staffers want to be engaged and to feel that their efforts make a difference. Staff members who are not included will feel estranged, and that will be reflected in their work habits.

Board members often don't realize the awkward situations and possible conflicts they can create. Acting in good faith, they can naively intrude on and interrupt office culture. They need to be given proper guidance.

Michelle is on her Reform temple's finance committee. As a member of this committee, she is entitled to receive financial reports. But rather than contact the office administrator and request that information, she calls the bookkeeper directly. "It's easier and more direct," she reasons. The bookkeeper is delighted with the social contact and appreciates the opportunity to be of service. When the administrator learns that this is occurring, she feels undermined and frustrated. Information is being disseminated without her knowledge and staff's work has been interrupted. How can this situation be resolved?

In order to preserve proper channels of authority and priorities without offending anyone, the better response to inappropriate interruptions would be to acknowledge the request, briefly explain the chain of command, and establish appropriate follow-up.

"I would love to, but I need to clear it with the administrator." "I'm sorry. I can't make calls for you until I complete a number of other tasks that need to be accomplished before the end of the day. Would you mind if I addressed that tomorrow?"

Understanding expectations and following the chain of command are essential to helping board and staff members grasp how to interact with one another.

Both staff and board need to understand the chain of command. It must be made clear that the senior staff person has the responsibility of monitoring staff-board interactions. Senior staff need to be prepared to assuage injured feelings, protect staff, and at the same time address and correct inappropriate board member behavior. Senior staff also need to monitor and ensure that criticism of volunteers' behavior does not openly occur in the office.

Board members have been known to become heavy-handed, make unreasonable demands, and lose perspective. Their behaviors can unwittingly intensify the staff's negative feelings.

I once had to ask my FJMC lay president to forbid certain board members from calling the office and speaking to staff. While the organization is responsible for integrating volunteers into the culture as smoothly as possible, it doesn't always work. An overbearing board member usually fades away, but it takes time.

Reinforcing the Chain

Understanding expectations and following the chain of command are essential to helping board and staff members grasp how to interact with one another. Too often, simple things like providing each member of the board with a written explanation or chart detailing staff's responsibility and indicating to whom requests should be directed are omitted from board orientation materials. A written document specifying office flow, which is on occasion reinforced by the president, may also help ensure that "efficiency" and "courtesy" are bywords of both board and staff.

Lay leadership and senior staff must remember that staff cannot be taken for granted and, like rank-and-file volunteers, need cultivation and nurturing. Board sensitivity is part of the overall approach to board-staff relations and has to be considered a necessary part of the organization's culture. Successful lay-professional relationships can boost productivity, increase volunteer self-esteem, and attract future staff members. Good staff relations is a valuable asset that should not be overlooked.

Talking Points

- What actions do lay leadership in your organization take to make staff feel appreciated?

- How is the internal chain of command in your organization communicated to the board? How well is it enforced?

- What strategies does your organization have in place to address issues that arise between lay leadership and staff?

- What instructions does your organization offer to help board members interact appropriately and effectively with staff?

- How do senior staff in your organization model ways to improve communication with each other, with your board, and with the staff?

6

THE COMMITTEE

Where the Rubber
Meets the Road

Committee work may be the most exciting or the least challenging role a volunteer can take on. It all depends on how the organization regards committee work. If leadership thinks of committees as groups of people who make things happen, the organization can attract and retain serious volunteers. However, you can be sure of a different result if the institution projects a message that work assigned to committees is of little importance.

How many times have you sat in a board meeting and heard someone say, "We shouldn't be doing this—it's committee work"? That may indeed be the case; some work is definitely better handled in committee. Boards can often make better use of their time by focusing on vision, goals, policy, and strategy as opposed to tactics or implementation details. But boards must be careful not to fall into the mismanagement trap in which they retain control over every substantive decision. Board work is by no means inherently more important than committee work.

Disparaging remarks by board members about how committees function or implying that certain committees are insignificant reflect a lack of understanding of the nature of volunteerism and undermine effective board-committee interactions. Consider the confusion that could occur in the absence of a committee of High Holy Day ushers or how a building could look if the building committee weren't functioning. The nature of their work may be different, but boards and committees often share a common process and common goals.

Boards need to focus on vision, policy, and strategy to ensure that goals are clearly set, needed income is available, and the organization functions as it should. Boards concentrate on understanding the larger picture, such as the organization's purpose, image, staffing, and future expansion. Boards think about policy and strategy. Committees think about how to improve specific areas and provide boards with the information necessary to make decisions based on a broader policy perspective.

Here's how it might work: A longstanding international membership organization has ceased to grow. It is currently organized on a club or chapter basis. People join clubs or local affiliates, which are part of larger regional bodies. These, in turn, report to an international board of directors. The leadership team—the board—concerned about the situation, forms a committee to investigate possible solutions. The committee determines that a new category of membership should be created that allows people who live outside an affiliate's designated area to become "individual members." The committee presents its recommendations to the board. The board amends its bylaws to allow this to happen and adopts most of the committee's recommendations. The board then creates a second committee to develop an implementation plan. That plan is subsequently accepted and funded. Within a year the organization begins to attract new members.

> Boards think about policy and strategy. Committees think about how to improve specific areas and provide boards with the information necessary to make larger decisions.

Committees and boards operate similarly but with different foci. Each has a chair, each needs to consider succession planning, and each operates with restrictions and within a specified time frame. Most important, each requires a specific vision, and each has goals to achieve. If you keep in mind their similarities, the differences between them need not become a problem.

Committee work is not necessarily menial work, but it must be done within a specific time frame to meet previously determined goals. Professional and lay leadership need to develop and transmit a clear understanding of the differences in function between the board and the committees.

THE MEANING OF MENIAL

Most leaders assume that there are great differences between people who gravitate toward membership, adult education, or social action committees and those who choose to serve on building, hospitality, or welcoming committees. In other words, some do important work and some do menial work—and those who perform the menial tasks are somehow less intelligent or skilled.

Accepting the notion that some committees handle "menial work" weakens committees and creates the false impression that those serving on certain committees simply have limited abilities. True, some people feel more comfortable or more challenged on committees that reflect their interests or abilities. But what about the brain surgeon who enjoys working in the kitchen? The college professor who needs the downtime and enjoys an occasional schmooze as a welcoming committee usher at Shabbat services? They're certainly not people of limited ability.

The bottom line is that every committee functions more effectively if its members feel appreciated and feel like part of a larger team working toward predetermined goals. Likewise, committees need to reevaluate themselves on a regular basis.

Achievement-oriented language, direction, and motivation are the bywords of a positive culture.

Committees must constantly strive to do better. The saying, "If it's not broken, don't fix it" reflects a regressive attitude that contradicts the reality that we live in a world of constant change. It's a negative attitude that should be replaced with its positive counterpart: "How can we do it better?"

Achievement-oriented language, direction, and motivation are the bywords of a positive culture. And a positive culture attracts more volunteers than a culture dedicated to preserving the status quo.

MAKING THE LEAP

Successful committee work does not necessarily lead to a position on the board. A board member might chair a specific committee, and committee members may be encouraged to serve on other committees. But a change in responsibilities and successful completion of committee assignments should not always be viewed as a stepping-stone to a seat on the board.

The common perception is that the not-for-profit world is an ascending ladder toward ever greater responsibility and status. That model is not necessarily best for an organization. If the culture (that is, the leadership) assumes that a successful committee person deserves a seat on the board, the leadership could elevate this person in a manner that does not undermine the committee structure. If, however, a message is transmitted that a committee post is valued as highly as a place on the board, it becomes easier to develop a more detailed portrait of the qualities and skills best suited for each position. This scenario creates stronger boards and more vibrant committees.

VISION PRECEDES MOTIVATION

Professional and lay leaders need to inspire their boards and committees to complete their designated tasks by providing participants with a long-range vision of how and why their work is important to the organization. Too often, committee chairs are simply told to increase membership, do public relations, or create a leadership development effort without the proper motivation. This omission undermines the strength and vigor of committees and fosters a two-tiered volunteer structure that compromises organizational effectiveness.

Leadership must remember that one of the key elements in running a successful volunteer organization is motivation. Yet leaders too often assume that their committee or board members are sufficiently motivated and understand what they need to know. They assume that people understand what has to be accomplished. They may. But that does not preclude the need for a reality check.

THE DANGER OF ASSUMPTIONS

A member of a synagogue approached me not too long ago with a question about his twenty-something daughter who was seriously involved with a non-Jewish man. He asked if he should invite the young man to a Passover Seder. I replied that if the daughter was indeed serious about her suitor, it would be better to integrate the young man into the family than to shun him.

The father countered with a response that I found somewhat confusing.

"But my mother-in-law is a survivor. How will she feel if her granddaughter brings home a non-Jewish man?"

"Who is more important to your future family relationship?" I asked.

"My daughter, of course," he responded. "But why couldn't she have found someone who's Jewish? She knows how important this is to me."

"Have you told her how important it is to you?" I asked.

"Well, she knows how important it is. I sent to her to Jewish day school, to Jewish summer camps, and to Israel. She knows!"

"Have you told her?" I repeated. "What do you think she thinks you think?"

"That she should marry Jewish."

"No," I answered. "I think she thinks that you love her and want what's best for her. Go tell her what else is important to you."

Get my point? Assume nothing. It's always better to clearly articulate your needs, concerns, and hopes. Leadership can't effectively lead if it operates on unexpressed assumptions. Just as the father should not have assumed that his daughter knew how he felt about her choice of a prospective husband, so, too, leaders need to remember that lay volunteers need to hear the leader's message articulated clearly. Repeating it from time to time drives it home. It works like motivation. Imparting information and motivating people are ongoing tasks.

> Assume nothing. It's always better to clearly articulate your needs, concerns, and hopes.

A similar pattern occurs with boards of directors when leadership neglects to motivate them.

I received a phone call from a hazzan who had been serving a congregation for twenty-seven years. The day after I had met with a group of men to help them organize a men's club, he called to thank me for my presentation and to tell me that it was the best meeting he had attended in twenty-seven years. I laughed and asked why. "It wasn't about budgets and it wasn't about logistics. It was about ideas and what the people in attendance could do to change the nature of their community. I want to be a member of your club," he said before he hung up.

SEPARATE IDENTITIES, EQUAL VALUE

Successful organizations take an expansive view of their culture. Both board and committee members are understood as groups of people who need to be motivated and empowered and who consider themselves as interlocking entities, contributing equally to the entire organizational enterprise. This creates a balanced platform that motivates both groups of volunteers.

In a previous chapter I mentioned that board positions are often filled by people who lack the qualifications to serve properly, despite the leadership's best efforts to prevent this. If the organization's culture treats both committees and boards with equal respect and value, committee members will feel fulfilled in that role and won't necessarily desire to seek positions on the board.

In one of my former synagogue positions, I decided that the congregation needed an active adult education program. The current adult education committee consisted of two people who arranged for an annual memorial lecture. It was obvious that people's intellectual needs weren't being met. An opportunity to involve dozens of synagogue members in adult education activities was being wasted. I reasoned that more involved congregants would translate into a more active community. With the synagogue president's guidance and my senior colleague's acquiescence, I assembled a committee, developed a proposal, and brought it to the board for approval.

I recruited a committee of six people, each one representing a different social group within the synagogue, who agreed to meet at my home once a month for three or four months. The meetings were substantive, intellectually challenging, and fun. I served wine and fruit at each meeting to lighten the mood, make everyone feel at home, and lessen the sense that these gatherings were all about "work."

> Board-committee relationships need not be complicated when clear lines of communication are established early on.

The group decided to create a mini-university called the "School in Shul." The program consisted of eight courses meeting four consecutive Wednesday evenings. Classes were divided into two periods, separated by a fifteen-minute coffee break. The high point of the semester would be a weekend scholar-in-residence program.

We developed a budget, decided what to charge people, and received a commitment for free printing of a brochure from a congregant who was delighted to be asked. But we still needed a sponsor or synagogue financing to cover the scholar's stipend. We also needed the board to sign off on the project.

All the committee members believed our plan was solid and assured of success. Still, we were nervous about how this proposal would be received by the board. So we put together a series of positions and strategies for achieving our goal.

With all that, we still came close to being voted down by the board on the grounds that, as the policymaking body, it had yet to officially determine if the adult education effort was needed in the first place. Had the president made this fact clear from the beginning and provided the committee with proper guidelines before we reached our decisions, we could have been working in sync.

The board, acting as a think tank and policymaking body, would have concluded that a strong adult education program was required, it would have allocated the needed funds, and it would have placed a person in charge of constituting the committee and developing the program. The committee, having received all necessary guidelines, would have created the initiative.

Instead, by circumventing the board, the president risked a devastating and demoralizing experience for newly motivated volunteers. Being forced to bring a proposal back to the board to request funding after all our work had been completed set up an adversarial situation that almost undermined the project. Board-committee relationships need not be complicated when clear lines of communication are established early on. When boards and committees work in tandem, it creates a spirit of cooperation and dedication that spreads throughout the institution.

Talking Points

- How are your organization's committees perceived by the organizational culture? How could that perception be improved?

- Are any stigmas attached to serving on a committee in your organization? If so, how could you eradicate those stigmas?

- Does your organization's board undermine committees? If so, how? What could be done to remedy that situation?

- How could you strengthen committee-board cooperation in your organization?

7

THE NOMINATING COMMITTEE

My Way or God's Way?

One at a time, each at his or her own pace, they ascend the stairs, shed their coats, and enter the room. It is any room anywhere, but the moment all of them are seated, an image comes to mind of seedy-looking gentlemen sitting around a simple table in a darkened room lit by a single bulb suspended from the ceiling and playing cards. The cards are dealt and people's fates are sealed. The future of the organization is determined. The nominating committee is in session.

People seeking office live in fear of nominating committees. They would rather risk the organization president's ire than offend a person who sits on that exalted committee, and for good reason. Nominating committee decisions determine both the volunteer's and the organization's future.

Scott is an aspiring volunteer officer of an international organization. He is invited to attend a high-level meeting with leaders from affiliates throughout the world. Before the meeting, the president of his organization takes him aside and cautions him not to say anything during the meeting—no suggestions, no comments. Just listen and learn. So Scott quietly observes how the organization's leadership interacts and responds to situations.

Scott is an independent businessperson. He is used to making serious financial decisions that affect the lives of hundreds of people on a regular basis. He disagrees with the manner in which the leadership of his organization operates, but he has been restrained, reined in. If he speaks out, he will never achieve a leadership position.

Scott is a victim of his organization's culture. He understands that if he wishes to ascend the organizational ladder, he will need to be a team player. If he is too assertive, he might step on someone's toes and, as a result, would never fulfill his goals. Scott has a choice: He can follow his president's advice, he can decide that this is not the organization for him, or he can speak his mind and risk never reaching a leadership position he has his heart set on. Scott is poised to become a slave to the nominating committee.

Of course, not all nominating committees function as if they had popped out of an Elizabethan novel. Many are exemplary. But too many nominating committees for synagogues and local, regional, or national organizations operate like self-serving fiefdoms, wielding power like a sledgehammer, and putting volunteers in an awkward—sometimes untenable—situation.

Nominating committees are usually governed by bylaws. In their absence, or when they have been misplaced or forgotten, or when weak leadership is in place, the institution's oral tradition—that is, what they remember—prevails. Organizations with weak structures have a tendency to function without or in violation of bylaws. It isn't unusual for a small not-for-profit organization, synagogue, or organization chapter to be governed through a combination of convenience and its oral tradition.

THE POINT OF BYLAWS

Les became the regional president of an international organization that had seen better days. His competition for president was nonexistent; he was the only person who would accept the job. Before his election, he attended a regional training seminar and was presented with a regional presidents' manual containing the organization's bylaws and constitution. Les owns a business, has a family, and is active in his synagogue. He simply never found the time to read the bylaws.

Under Les's guidance, a fifteen-year decline in membership and fundraising was reversed in the region. He began to build a new board of directors and cultivate new leaders. During his two years in office, he called on the organization's central office whenever he faced a procedural question. Six months before his term ended he had no idea how to select a successor. He had never looked at the bylaws, and the oral tradition, the institutional memory, had been lost.

> How the nominating committee works with its incoming administration is an important indication of organizational culture.

THE DARKROOM MENTALITY

It is common practice for immediate past presidents of organizations to chair nominating committees. How the nominating committee works with its incoming administration is an important indication of organizational culture. Nominating committees can engage in either an open or a closed process. Closed committees assume that they know what is best for the organization. While they might solicit input from the incoming leadership, it is very clear, at least to them, that decisions within their purview will be theirs and people will learn the results at the appropriate time. This closed process—sometimes referred to as a darkroom mentality—is indicative of a committee that views itself as an independent body. This "lockbox" attitude reflects organizational weakness and cultural elitism.

Nominating committees should operate in an open and honest fashion.

A number of years ago a major international organization held a board meeting in San Antonio, Texas. The nominating committee wanted to upgrade the leadership of the organization and recommended people for office who were more sophisticated and wealthier than the current leadership. The nominating committee's plans were revealed in an untimely fashion, and charges of corruption filled the meeting room. Half of the current board resigned. The incident is recorded in the minutes of the organization under the heading "Remember the Alamo." Nominating committees can operate with the best of intentions, but if they function without the open cooperation of their boards, they run the risk of causing a great deal of damage.

OUT WITH THE OLD ...

Nominating committees can also be structured in ways that limit organizational growth. When nominating committees are composed almost exclusively of past leaders, the organization reinforces its existing culture and limits its exposure to new ideas.

When the nominating committee works with its incoming president in an open manner, regardless of who will receive subsequent nominations, this approach to volunteerism and organizational life embraces change and can potentially minimize conflict and damage.

Barbara, the incoming president of Temple Beth-el, had a strong desire to increase her synagogue's membership, and to accomplish this she needed a strong team of leaders. Thankfully, the chair of the nominating committee asked what her hopes and aims were going to be in her administration and which people would she like to work with. The nominating committee gave Barbara's goals serious consideration when they worked on the slate. Barbara didn't get everything she wanted because the committee had a broader vision of the synagogue. But she was provided with a team that could help her do the job.

Nominating committees also need to be cognizant of volunteers' feelings. Thoughtful committees will develop strategies to involve the volunteer who will not be renominated in order to lessen the inevitable disappointment that ensues. Concerned committees will estimate the potential loss of a volunteer's efforts if the announcement is made public too soon, will consider whether the

> Thoughtful committees will develop strategies to involve the volunteer who will not be renominated in order to lessen the inevitable disappointment that ensues.

volunteer may no longer fulfill her responsibilities upon learning of their decisions, and will develop an appropriate strategy to maintain that volunteer's involvement.

Rachel, chair of the nominating committee at Temple Sinai, had decided in concert with her committee that two of the five vice presidents would not be renominated as officers because they had not fulfilled the synagogue's expectations. Unfortunately, these individuals also chaired a number of important committees, and if they withdrew from those positions or those committees fell short of predetermined goals, the synagogue would fail to meet its budget.

Rachel met with the incoming president, shared the nominating committee's concerns, and encouraged the president-elect to meet with these people individually to explain that, regardless of the nominating committee's decision, he wanted them to assume a major role during his term of office. The incoming president followed her advice. Both people were buoyed by these conversations and continued to serve even after they learned that they would not be renominated as vice presidents.

I remember when the chair of an organization's nominating committee was supposed to announce the new slate at a board retreat. The chair had assured the executive director and the incoming and outgoing presidents that the people not being renominated would be handled with the utmost sensitivity. It was a Saturday evening. It was downtime; people were drinking beer and eating chips. The football playoffs were on television, and some of the men had chosen to change into their team jerseys. In the middle of the game, the nominating committee chair walked into the room, touched three people on the shoulder, and asked them to step outside the room for a moment. He thought he was being sensitive. Once they had accompanied him outside the room he told them they were being dumped. It took three months to repair the damage. Sometimes it is necessary for the nominating committee to share a plan with the incoming president and senior staff that demonstrates how they are going to attempt to minimize hurt feelings. I know of several rabbis who insist on seeing a written plan explaining how people are going to be told that they are being rejected before the nominating committee acts.

> It is the rare nominating committee that realizes the bylaws were not handed down at Sinai and need to be revised regularly.

LOOKING TO THE FUTURE

Nominating committees are also key to determining whether an organization is structured for growth. If the committee is future-directed but constantly finds itself feeling limited by the existing bylaws, it should share this with the incoming board. It is the rare nominating committee that realizes the bylaws were not handed down at Sinai and need to be revised regularly.

Synagogue boards must understand that elevating people to a high rank raises their expectations: "If I can become vice president, why not president?" Some synagogues have too many vice presidents, many of whom lack the necessary skills to serve in a presidential capacity. This can create a situation in which people's feelings are hurt every few years because they will not be renominated and people with the necessary presidential qualities could be sidelined because it appears that a large of number of vice presidents are already poised to rise to the top spot. A forward-thinking nominating committee realizes that situations like this foster tension and undercut the opportunity for growth.

> Nominating committees need to realize that a successful volunteer culture constantly attracts and integrates new volunteers.

Nominating committees need to adopt a long-range vision of their mission, coupled with the realization that a successful volunteer culture constantly attracts and integrates new volunteers. For organizations to accomplish this, a vehicle to retain existing and former talent must be created. Nominating committees should review the organizational structure to ascertain if the modus operandi currently in place is helping or hindering organizational growth.

It is a great honor to serve on the board of at least one major international Jewish organization. As a result, organizational volunteers seek to become board members rather than officers. Board members, like committee members, of any not-for-profit organization can fulfill a number of critical roles and be accorded appropriate status, allowing space for policymakers and long-range planners to assume positions of high office.

Nominating committees stand at the apex of an organization's structure. The choices they make can move an organization backward or forward or simply maintain the status quo. If a nominating committee adopts a long-range view, it can stimulate thinking that results in expanded institutional activity and additional volunteers. At the same time, it must challenge officers to create language that counters the climate of elitism that often permeates volunteer organizations.

Talking Points

- Are the bylaws of your organization current? If not, what plans are in the works to update them?

- Does your nominating committee stimulate or inhibit your organization's volunteers? How could your nominating committee strengthen the commitment of your volunteers?

- How well does your nominating committee represent your institution?

- How has your nominating committee been structured to encourage change and growth? If it hasn't, how could it be restructured to be more forward-looking?

8

CULTIVATING LEADERSHIP
Balancing the Seesaw

It is the ongoing responsibility of professional and lay leadership to identify, target, cultivate, and nurture future leadership. Succession planning is crucial for the synagogue and small institution as well as for the large international organization. In an ideal world, both lay leaders and professionals embody the same skill sets. The reality is that the lay-professional balance will continuously shift like a seesaw, depending on situations and people's strengths and weaknesses. In spite of these differences, if both lay leaders and professionals adhere to certain basic guidelines, their differences can be successfully mediated.

It's up to the professionals to adjust and adapt their skills to the needs of their laity, but identifying, targeting, involving, and cultivating future leaders is a responsibility that is shared equally. Sharing responsibilities is a little bit different in the synagogue, where lay leadership rarely substitutes for the rabbi. However, when it comes to cultivating leadership, a team effort is necessary.

THE DOWNSIDE

Sometimes professionals can upset the balance. Ensconced professionals have a tendency to gloss over or forget that it is their responsibility to adapt themselves and their skills in ways that nurture and enhance their lay leadership. Too often their vision and understanding of an organization's needs or their desire to move the organization in a specific direction cause them to undermine current and developing lay leadership. Consider the following examples:

Identifying, targeting, involving, and cultivating future leaders is a responsibility that is shared equally. When it comes to cultivating leadership, a team effort is necessary.

Max served as CEO of a local federation for more than twenty years. For all that time, he monitored the same budget, attended regular and repetitive board meetings, and staffed the same committees. But he was bored. He had reached a point in his career where he would rather be developing new projects than guiding his emerging lay leadership. Rather than taking the time to explain the budget process and meeting agendas to engage his leadership in this process, he simply presented the information to them, outlined possible pitfalls, and moved ahead.

Rabbi Z. served the same congregation for thirty years. Five years ago he was granted a life contract. He was very involved in a number of international organizations dedicated to improving the lot of world Jewry. The previous year he was away from his congregation for seven weeks, working on behalf of the Jewish people. It was important work, but so was his congregation. Rabbi Z. had forgotten who paid his salary.

Roberta led an organization that helped communities grow. Her community-based organizational and advocacy skills empowered volunteers to strengthen their communities. For years she and her leadership were stymied by the lack of respect their organization received. Out of desperation, she and her current lay leadership took a big risk. They purchased property in Israel with the hope of creating a community-based leadership program in the Holy Land. They hoped this could become a symbol around which their North American affiliates would rally and generate support. Unfortunately, they misjudged the strength of their connection to those affiliates, whose members wanted them to focus on initiatives in the United States and didn't have the desire or the resources to contribute to a project abroad. As a result, they placed their organization in a precarious financial situation.

In the first situation, Max's boredom and desire to alleviate it prompted him to place his personal needs above those of the organization. The constant round of meetings and budgets clouded his judgment and pushed him to attempt to plow through the process as quickly as possible. Like a teacher who has taught the same material for too long, he allowed the nature of the material instead of the challenge of communicating it to govern his actions. Had he viewed the daily cycle as an opportunity to cultivate leadership, he might have retained his enthusiasm and created a vehicle that challenged and developed future leadership. He simply lost his professional balance.

Having lost perspective, Max lost respect for his lay leaders. Rather than view his interactions with them as an opportunity to both learn and guide, he instead came to see them as obstacles, preventing him from accomplishing the exciting things he dreamed of. At the same time, his long tenure lulled the lay leaders into complacency, and they no longer questioned him. It's as if they had forgotten that he worked for them.

Rabbi Z. took his congregation for granted; he also forgot that leadership development is an ongoing process. If he wasn't attentive, his community would suffer. The same can also be said for Roberta's situation. In each case, a desire to raise an organization's profile and prestige overrode the organization's mission—service to a particular constituency.

Lay leaders are often equally as guilty. When this occurs, senior staff are faced with the decision of either capitulating to an overbearing leader or getting fired. Organizations that have lost a sense of their mission or have squandered their political capital or good will in the community face a serious dilemma, requiring a lay leadership training iniative to set things right.

THE UPSWING: CORRECTING INSTITUTIONAL IMBALANCE

Well-balanced organizations understand that leadership training must be integral to their culture. Most organizations have a tendency to view leadership training as a separate track or occasional occurrence rather than part and parcel of the organization itself. Organizations that reflect these attitudes toward leadership development condemn themselves to a status quo future at best.

> The culture that defines, promotes, and demonstrates that leadership development is an integral part of its culture makes a statement about the aims and goals of the organization.

In an attempt to attract young people and cultivate new leadership, numerous secular and religious organizations have developed young leadership tracks, young couples clubs, or similar programs. Most of these efforts last for a few years and then lose their momentum. The efforts fail because the young people involved were not integrated into positions of leadership and no ongoing effort was made to target and train new generations of up-and-coming leaders.

If organizational leaders accept that targeting and nurturing future leadership form an integral part of the organization's culture, then the manner in which potential volunteers and leaders are approached can substantially change. The culture that defines, promotes, and demonstrates that leadership development is a top priority makes a statement about the aims and goals of the organization. If this process is carried out properly, future leaders will emerge and their enthusiasm and fresh ideas will infuse the organization with energy for years to come.

THE JOY OF VOLUNTEERISM: DON'T FORGET THE "F" WORD

Institutional cultures need to demonstrate compassion, trust, and flexibility when seeking to attract and working with volunteers. Let's not overlook the importance of fun.

The "f" word—fun—is surprisingly lacking in the rhetoric of most volunteer organizations. We often hear words like "important" or "meaningful" or phrases such as "You can help to make a difference." But rarely the "f" word. Rather than say "fun," most senior volunteers and professionals will stress the feelings of satisfaction people derive from the successful completion of important tasks. However, unless they're having fun in the process, volunteers are not likely to stick around for any significant length of time.

Organizations sponsor social events as fundraisers and as tools to involve people. These activities are designed to provide enjoyment, but they aren't necessarily fun. Concerts and plays are enjoyable; indeed, they can often be a lot more. Dances and talent shows and auctions are entertaining, but they don't reflect the type of fun that is often needed to make something memorable.

Fun is a core value that needs to be taught to and embodied in both volunteer leadership and staff. It creates the proper volunteer environment by fostering involvement and relationships. Laughter is contagious. It is also a tool that allows us to admit personal and organizational weaknesses and strength. When properly used, it can project a message that "as important as we think we are or we would like to be, we also know that we are fallible human beings." When leaders, lay or professional, make others laugh or laugh at themselves, it creates an opportunity for engagement that encourages people to take a risks and come along for the ride.

> Fun is a core value that needs to be taught to and embodied in both volunteer leadership and staff.

Fun isn't about being a comedian or a person telling jokes. Fun isn't about sarcasm or inappropriate humor. Fun is about seizing a moment in a memorable way so that it changes a mood, excites people, and makes them feel that their lives are being touched. Fun is about being able to be serious and not take yourself too seriously. Fun is about being able to laugh at yourself.

In March 2009, ten members of three lay organizations in the Conservative Movement spent a weekend together to learn how they could better work with one another. It was a historic meeting with the goal of establishing workable, trusting relationships. The cultures of each organization were different, as were their products and services. Friday evening after services and dinner, some members of the group led a session of Jewish college bowl. The leader was more than a person who read questions, he was an engager; he brought the group together in laughter. People had fun, and the concerns and barriers between them began to melt. Making people laugh is serious business.

I remember one Sunday morning being stuck in a traffic jam with three volunteer leaders. We were driving from downtown Philadelphia to a meeting on the New Jersey shore and were tied up by a "Run for Cancer" event. The police told us to turn off our cars. We wouldn't be moving until the race was finished in about forty-five minutes. I surveyed the street; it was a gridlock situation. I exited the car, assessed the situation, and announced, "I can do something about this. We have to get out of here."

The group looked at me as if I were deranged.

"Watch me," I said.

I had to convince the drivers of two minivans, one bus, and two cars to back up in order for our driver to obtain sufficient space to creatively turn around and get us out of there. A number of other cars followed suit. Sometimes, leaders are expected to make miracles! If not miracles, meaningful moments.

My bold leadership gambit wasn't an "a-ha" moment that reflects a personal revelation. It was more of a "Ha! Ha!" moment. They laughed hysterically, forged deeper bonds of friendship, and remember that trip to this day. Hopefully, if a similar situation ever occurs in the future, they will step forward and make something happen.

STAY BALANCED, BE FLEXIBLE

To successfully attract potential leaders in volunteer community organizations, institutions need to demonstrate flexibility toward their members and chapters. Flexibility needs to be understood as a basic element of the organization's culture. Oftentimes in the past this hasn't been the case, but in a rapidly changing society, organizations need to be fluid. Institutional flexibility is one of a few key characteristics that can foster, attract, and retain future volunteers and leadership.

This can be extremely challenging for many not-for-profit organizations, because they tend to adhere to specific predetermined regulations, and the larger they become, the more corporately they behave. One of the unconscious goals of most not-for-profit organizations is to model themselves on their corporate counterparts. However, the volunteer world operates under a different set of guidelines. Leadership's desire to be viewed as an efficient, modern, and smoothly run organization can cause the organization to develop a callous and impersonal organizational style. Rules and procedures are important, but flexibility and sensitivity to people trump them all. The synagogue that understands that volunteering is in direct competition with the leisure-time market, which is completely flexible, and not the corporate world, has successfully positioned itself to attract volunteers and future leaders.

> Institutional flexibility is one of a few key characteristics that can foster, attract, and retain future volunteers and leadership.

Irv is one of a number of vice presidents of a major investment bank and simultaneously serves on the synagogue board of directors. He does his best to attend the board meetings, but has time for little else. He has expressed an interest in learning to read Hebrew, but between his work and family schedule, he can't find the time. His quality of life is suffering. One evening after a board meeting, Irv shared his feelings with his rabbi.

"I understand your dilemma, Irv. I really do. I wonder if there isn't some way we could find the time. My life is rather busy at certain times, too, and when I have a medical or legal question, I call my doctor or lawyer and meet with them on the phone. Do you think you could find twenty minutes a week to learn Hebrew by phone with me?"

Just as the rabbi was able to accommodate his schedule to address Irv's needs, synagogues and organizations must find ways to operate in a flexible fashion.

I have witnessed a number of instances where organizational affiliates have been stripped of their ties to the parent body because they were delinquent in paying dues. In most cases the affiliates were experiencing a temporary financial hardship. A flexible organization would work with them and demonstrate understanding and compassion. An inflexible one operates by the book, generating animosity that could lead to a severing of ties between the parent organization and the affiliate.

The B'nai Israel Synagogue, a prominent synagogue in the bedroom community of a major city, had been an ardent supporter of its umbrella organization for more than forty years. Last year its boiler unexpectedly failed, causing the synagogue to reassess its members and borrow funds from a bank. It appealed to the umbrella synagogue organization for a dues waiver, explaining that it would have difficulty meeting its $30,000 dues payment in the coming year. Synagogue leaders also requested a dues reduction for the current year and the year after. The request was denied, and the synagogue was placed on suspension until the full dues payment had been met.

The community eventually and grudgingly fulfilled its obligation. Their responsibility to the parent organization took precedence over their hardship and resentment. But the community suffered. Because they felt obligated to pay their dues to the parent organization, the congregation had less money available to engage a school educator and were forced to hire a person of lesser caliber than they would have liked. Their school attendance began a downward trend that took years to reverse.

A flexible institution would have granted the waiver and created an opportunity to increase volunteer commitment and identification with their organization. In this instance, the corporate attitude created a rift, rather than an opportunity. If an organization is to successfully attract leaders and build stronger ties with its affiliates, it must be responsive to their needs.

Leadership takes many forms. An organization that can accommodate its methods of operation to the special circumstances of its members will create a reservoir of goodwill that will be reflected in the values and commitment it inspires in its leaders and volunteers. A healthy organizational culture understands, supports, and responds proactively to its leadership and potential leadership when they encounter personal or professional situations that constrain their ability to manage effectively.

Tom will be elected international vice president of an organization at its annual convention in three months. Attending the convention will entail a significant expense. Tom has two children in college and a mother-in-law who recently fell ill and requires full-time nursing care. This past week Tom's car died, and it will have to be replaced. Tom feels overwhelmed and is reevaluating whether he can afford to attend the convention. The president of the organization calls Tom and tells him that he understands and sympathizes with his situation. He says that he values Tom's input and sees him as a key player in the future. He makes a point of telling Tom that he shouldn't be deterred by the convention expense; the organization will provide as much financial support as Tom needs to make it work for him. Tom will be a volunteer in that organization for the rest of his life.

The volunteer world is about people. People appreciate when they are treated with compassion and flexibility. The culture that demonstrates compassion and flexibility models this form of behavior. It is one of the keys to fostering future leadership.

TRUST, RISK,
AND MAKING THINGS HAPPEN

Demonstrating trust in a volunteer is as important as demonstrating compassion and flexibility. Leaders who trust their volunteers empower them to be leaders. Leaders who trust are willing to encourage others to take risks and are prepared to do everything they can to head off potential failure. Leaders who trust also recognize that not succeeding is different from failing. A successful leader—lay or professional—understands that people never fail as volunteers; they just haven't fully succeeded.

Trusting, being willing to take risks, modeling compassion, and being flexible are all crucial qualities, but the one that is most overlooked is the opportunity to create meaningful moments. While this is difficult to describe, if successful, it can simultaneously raise the volunteer bar and inspire others. As a leader in a volunteer or even a corporate setting, you are the one people instinctively expect to make things happen. Too often, people in positions of leadership fail to capitalize on this opportunity. They sense the opportunity, but hesitate to step forward and take the risk.

I remember at the World Zionist Congress of 2004 all the leaders of the Conservative/Masorti Movement were gathered together one morning to pray at Robinson's Arch, the part of the Western Wall in Jerusalem where Conservative Jews are allowed to gather for prayer. The group was composed of leaders from seventeen countries, but lacked a titular head. Some of the rabbis were waiting to be asked to lead the prayer service. Everyone was waiting for someone to ask one of them to assume the responsibility, and then a lay leader stood up, walked to the wall, and began to pray. He became the leader. Everyone—all the leaders, both great and small—followed his lead.

Leaders are supposed to make things happen. They are supposed to create new opportunities and find new ways to resolve crisis situations. Leaders don't have to be visionaries or charismatic personalities, but they do have to know when to seize the moment. They can foster a working, striving, committed atmosphere that promotes volunteerism, as long as they are not too harsh or too inflexible.

Leaders cannot lead by consensus. They need to take responsibility for their actions. People in positions of influence should see themselves as motivators of others and, as such, become coaches instead of micromanagers.

TARGETING AND CULTIVATING LEADERSHIP: THE LAY-PROFESSIONAL PARTNERSHIP

When it comes to targeting and developing future leadership, professionals and lay leaders have the same job and need to engage in the same process. Both need to acknowledge that a key aspect of their role is to look for likely potential leaders all the time. The rabbi who teaches a class or officiates at a life-cycle occasion is constantly exposed to potential volunteers and potential leaders. The congregation president or regional officer of a synagogue-based organization who visits local affiliates or who dines socially with new people has numerous opportunities to educate and engage future volunteers and potential leaders.

Too often, professional and lay leaders fail to take advantage of these opportunities. This usually happens because these leaders haven't thought through and committed to a predetermined process. The rabbi who teaches a class and the lay leader who meets new people at social occasions both must remember that the people they are meeting are potential volunteers and potential leaders! They need to assess the people with whom they are interacting and ask themselves whether these people have the ability to assume a leadership role in the community and whether they can be integrated into the organization's culture. They have to remember these people's names and follow up by asking a few questions about them. They need to share these names with their fellow leaders and compare notes. Finally, they should develop a specific strategy for engaging these prospective volunteers and potential leaders.

> Leaders are supposed to make things happen. They are supposed to create new opportunities and find new ways to resolve crisis situations.

The strategy for engaging volunteers is simple. It begins with a phone call and an invitation to get together. It continues at the meeting with an explanation of the organization's culture; its aims, objectives, strengths, and advantages; and the reason for the meeting. For example:

"Hello, Ruth. This is Chuck. I've been thinking about you and about a project I'm involved with. I thought it might be fun for us to work together. It won't take a lot of time, and it could have a really positive impact on the community. Can we meet for a cup of coffee so we can catch up and I can explain it?"

"Mike, what a coincidence meeting you on the street like this. Do you have moment? I've become involved in an interesting project with a small group of exciting people. We are from all walks of life, united in purpose. We would like to think that our little group can improve the lives of our frail elderly. Most of us don't have very much time, so we meet infrequently but think intensively. I'm sure you could contribute to our thinking and would enjoy spending time with us. What do you think?"

The exchange concludes with the leader creating an opportunity for both the prospective volunteer and the lay and professional leadership of the organization to take a risk. "We would appreciate it if you would meet a number of us for coffee next week. We would like to hear your impressions of our plan so far and the process we envision to bring this to fruition." This meeting will forge a path that the prospective volunteer or future leader will be able to navigate.

The culture of the organization is the breeding ground for the values it holds. A united and well-balanced lay-professional partnership promotes organizational growth. An organization should reflect its core values. For an organization to thrive in a rapidly changing society, its core values must include ongoing leadership and volunteer development, compassion, trust, flexibility, *and fun*. That kind of culture attracts and retains volunteers.

Talking Points

- How have the professionals in your organization adjusted and adapted their skills to meet the needs of their laity? What more can be done to make them more responsive?

- How well do your organization's goals mesh with your mission statement?

- How is the responsibility to cultivate future leaders shared among members of your organization?

- What is your organization's strategy for identifying and targeting future volunteers?

- How can your organization foster a feeling of trust between your leadership and your volunteer workforce?

- What steps can you take to encourage humor and a sense of fun in the day-to-day workings of your organization?

9

WHEN THINGS ARE JUST NOT WORKING

The Forever President and Other Problematic People

I remember visiting the president of one of the local FJMC chapters in South Florida a number of years ago. I was in my late thirties; he was in his early eighties. Our conversation began with my asking questions about his chapter: "Tell me about your chapter. What difficulties are you experiencing? What success have you had? What failures?"

I learned that he had been the chapter president for more than a decade. Being much younger and more naive, I immediately assumed that because I was the professional, I, of course, was the expert—a big mistake. I suggested that he should consider tendering his resignation. "Trust me," I said. "Leadership will come forward." The conversation went like this:

"You know, Rabbi, I've been president of my chapter for more than ten years."

"I think that's admirable, but don't you think you're doing your club a disservice? You're holding back development of new leadership, and we certainly can use a person with your abilities on a regional level."

"Resign? Resign! You don't understand, Rabbi. If I do that, everything will fall apart! Do you think I've been president for this long a time because I like it? I can't get anyone to follow me. My board is barely active. If it weren't for me, this chapter wouldn't exist. Believe me, no one else will take the job."

"Your board is barely active? Who runs the programs? Who orders the food and arranges for the speakers?"

"Well, I do, of course. I have a couple of friends who help out when I ask them, but they're not getting any younger."

"Neither are you. [Whoops! Another mistake.] Maybe you should resign. People will come forward."

"Rabbi, you're young. Trust me—I've been doing this for a long time. No one will take the job."

"How do you know? Maybe if you were seen as more of an advisor, or as someone who just didn't have the strength to do it anymore, new leadership would emerge."

Need I say that I failed miserably at convincing the gentleman to transfer the reins of leadership to someone else?

The issues surrounding the relinquishing of responsibilities and the ways to help volunteers do so are complicated. While it is preferable for a nominating committee to create a slate that designates and prepares future leadership, the reality is that nominating committees only exist if they are embodied in bylaws or organizational memory. Oftentimes, organizational memory is limited to two to three years, because people come and go or the organization never firmly established this protocol at the outset.

> Weak and newly formed institutions generally ignore issues like planning for volunteer leadership transition.

Weak organizations have a tendency to neglect history as well as bylaws (somehow they have been lost or haven't been read for a number of years), while newly formed organizations are usually concerned with solidifying their base and meeting existing needs. Weak and newly formed institutions generally ignore issues like planning for volunteer leadership transition.

Leadership transition needs to begin as soon as a new president takes office. In the situation I describe above, convincing this veteran to move on required long-term strategies and an acknowledgment that failure to easily dislodge him was perhaps as likely as success.

I attempted to salvage the meeting by redirecting my questions to his chapter's successes and failures. The failures, he was quick to point out, centered on the lack of people willing to come forward.

"I can't get people involved. People just don't want to become involved the way they used to, the way my generation did."

The president's responses told me a great deal about him and why his chapter was floundering. He used the word "I" repeatedly. He was incapable of separating the chapter's identity from his own.

I remember asking, "What were the most successful programs [he didn't think in terms of initiatives] the chapter offered in the past year?" He gleefully responded, while still bemoaning the fact that young men weren't joining and that the few who did were unwilling to take on leadership tasks: "Rabbi, we had a great program last month. We had the best attendance since the lecture on Social Security. We had a post-colostomy workshop."

Is it any wonder that he failed to attract younger men? As the father of a toddler at that time, I can assure you that this program wouldn't have attracted me or any of my peers.

RETIRING THE FOREVER PRESIDENT

How to work with and respond to volunteers who assume long-term possession of a position—I call them "forever presidents"—is an ongoing concern. While it may benefit an organization to have the same committed volunteers fulfill specific tasks over the short and even the long term, this is not the case when it comes to the volunteer leadership team. If the goal is to build volunteer involvement and to train a succession of leaders, the presence of entrenched people in leadership roles presents a serious stumbling block.

An example where having entrenched volunteers can work well is an annual blood drive led by individuals who make that their niche and are committed to running it year after year. This might satisfy their desire to volunteer, and asking them to step aside not only would hurt their feelings but would compromise the organization's programs. But nothing and no one last forever. These individuals must accept people who are trained as designated successors. Life is unpredictable. Illness or some other reason likely will prevent long-time volunteers from carrying out their self-appointed mission at some point.

> Forever presidents linger forever. They're like not-for-profit organizations that become entrenched bureaucracies and endure long past the time whan their mission has been fulfilled.

The lifetime men's club president poses a different dilemma than the entrenched volunteer who runs one program. Yet convincing the forever president to cede the reins of power may be turned into an opportunity for strengthening an organization. Doing so requires lay and professional leadership to assess their institution's current functioning and consider how to improve it. The resulting vision presents an opportunity to engage the perennial leader in a discussion of why the organization is not growing. With the discussion shifted away from the individual and toward the institution, the forever president may be persuaded to facilitate change.

Some organizations ignore the forever president situation because they are not willing to take the necessary time to address it. They are satisfied with the status quo. Other times leadership recognizes that a weak leader or a weak affiliate is having a detrimental impact on the larger organization. The first step toward rectifying this situation is establishing a committee to consider the long-term implications of allowing this situation to fester.

That committee needs to ask, "Can we make a distinction between an individual who holds an elected office for a long-term period and a longtime committee chair, and if so, how do they differ? Is it in the organization's interest to allow an individual to retain a longstanding position, and if not, how can this situation be rectified?"

Forever presidents linger forever. They're like not-for-profit organizations that become entrenched bureaucracies and endure long past the time whan their mission has been fulfilled. Yet, in the still-to-be-written Bible for not-for-profit organizations, I am confident that the God of not-for-profits would never permit, let alone encourage, organizational immortality or forever presidents.

There are times when it is in the long-term interest of the institution to temporarily dissolve a dependent organization, such as a committee, in order to create an atmosphere in which future leadership can emerge. There are times when senior leadership needs to confront the forever president and inform him that he will be retired or moved into another area in the near future.

Not too long ago, I spoke to a congregational president who was concerned that the men's club was not supporting the temple financially and had ceased to offer summer camp scholarships to its youth. The club was not lacking in funds. I advised him to meet with the club members and explain to them that this was one of their primary obligations within the synagogue and that failure to meet those obligations would result in their being dissolved.

I can think of a number of situations where the forever president agreed to step down after being engaged in serious conversation with synagogue leadership. The forever president remains president simply because no one has made the effort to address the situation.

WORKING WITH THE
DIFFICULT VOLUNTEER

Just as a strategy is needed to work with a volunteer who refuses to relinquish a position, additional strategies are required to work with volunteers who have difficulty working with others. Not-for-profits need volunteers, but how do they address the volunteer who has trouble fitting in?

The institution that fails to act because it fears the possible consequences is responding from a position of weakness. A healthy organization has the courage to move forward as it deems necessary.

When it comes to the difficult volunteer, there are two different philosophies. One school posits, "Cut your losses. It was a mistake involving her. It's not going to be worth the time to correct the situation, and sometimes people's feelings will get hurt. Accept the inevitable and get rid of her."

The other view reminds us, "A place can always be found for a good volunteer, at least for a short period. We just need to find the right motivational language and position." It is not uncommon for a person to be promoted to a different position or be offered a special type of recognition in order to remedy a situation in which a talented individual is not functioning well. To a certain extent "kicking them upstairs" might be a useful short-term intervention. In the long run, it could also minimize damage and preserve organizational integrity.

A responsible volunteer organization always attempts to hold on to even less-than-successful volunteers. I suspect that this is because we realize that everyone has something to contribute, and that everyone can make a difference in some way. When a situation arises and a volunteer or a volunteer's position is at risk, staff and lay leadership need to intervene. We always hope the intervention will be successful. Unfortunately, sometimes that's just wishful thinking.

Organizations and senior leadership are often hesitant to dismiss volunteers. They tend to avoid direct action because they are afraid of losing the volunteer or perhaps the volunteer's friends. Senior leaders need to be cognizant of these feelings but not swayed by them. The institution that fails to act because it fears the possible consequences is responding from a position of weakness. A healthy organization has the courage to move forward as it deems necessary.

The manner in which lay and professional leaders respond to these difficult and awkward situations is extremely important because the context of the responses will always be viewed as a reflection of the organization's culture and values. If leadership responds autocratically or in a manner that doesn't reflect its culture, that culture can be jeopardized.

Interventions rarely need to take place immediately.

The rabbi and congregation president are awakened one morning by a call from the police. The synagogue has been desecrated. Vandals have painted swastikas on the building. The rabbi and president quickly confer and decide to paint over the damage before the community finds out.

This was probably not the wisest response. Leaving the swastika on the building for a brief period would have created an opportunity for community education and cooperation. The community could have come together to paint over the swastika. What seemed like a situation that demanded immediate action was, in fact, better suited for a well-thought-out response.

Organizations are usually more effective if they take the following advice: "Don't respond instinctively. Don't respond immediately."

Almost every situation can wait for and is better off with a thoughtful response. The scenarios that follow reflect potential crises in the making. If poorly handled, each could result in a failure to accomplish predetermined goals that could rupture an institution. None of them requires an immediate response, and all of them deserve a thoughtful one.

How should leadership respond to people who have difficulty working in a group or who exhibit divisive behavior?

The Overinvested Volunteer

"I'm sorry. I just can't let go of it. I know that if the board votes the way it's leaning, it will be making a major mistake."

Overinvested volunteers become frustrated when their advice is not followed. Their assessment of the situation may even be correct. But once the board has made its decision, it's time to move on.

An information technology committee in a synagogue was asked to recommend a new computer network system. The committee consisted of a number of engineers and computer mavens, each of whom approached the task differently. After months of discussion, they still couldn't agree on the proper technology for the synagogue. Their disagreement set the project back months, and eventually the president was forced to make the decision for them. Several people on the committee probably wondered, "Why won't they listen to me?"

A mature, seasoned organizational volunteer might simply shrug off the decision by saying, "I did the best I could. Sometimes you get what you want, sometimes you don't. I'll learn to live with their decision."

But volunteers who are overly invested in the process become frustrated, alienated, and angry. They can't let go of their negative feelings and they see the rejection of their recommendations as personal failure. To continue to function as successful volunteers, they must learn to sublimate their negative feelings into positive actions. The job of the leader (lay or professional) is to help them make this transition. The injured parties need to realize that this is not about them—or anyone else for that matter. It's not about winning or losing; it's about relationships and working together for the greater good.

> The successful intervention is one that praises the volunteer's dedication and redirects it toward a form of greater service.

The successful intervention is one that praises the volunteer's dedication and redirects it toward another form of service. Unfortunately, there are also times when the overinvested volunteer just will not let go and the intervention fails.

The Overbearing Volunteer

"You've got to get rid of him. He's a moron! I call him and tell him what to do. He agrees to everything—the timetable, the language to use—and then he does something completely different. Please find me someone else to work with!"

Sometimes leaders need to consider which volunteer is the problem. Is someone really a moron, or could the mentor be the one at fault? Could the lay leader's evaluation of the volunteer be correct, or is the problem being caused by the one who's complaining?

Failure to properly mentor another volunteer can reveal a tragic flaw in developing leadership. It might demonstrate the limits to which a volunteer can rise, learn, and remain part of the organization's culture.

The Volunteer Who Intimates Others

"I don't understand how a person as competent as you can do everything wrong! That's not the way to get something done. If it had been my job, it would have been twice as successful."

Is it even possible for leaders to find a place for an individual who belittles others?

The Socially Inept Volunteer

Melanie is a gifted, creative thinker. She writes poetry and is much more intellectually sophisticated than many of the volunteers in leadership positions, but she is thin-skinned and has trouble focusing.

"I know what I'm supposed to do when the meeting starts, and then someone asks a question and I think about it, and that leads me to think about something else, and once someone makes a little joke, I can't keep myself from responding," she says.

What options are available to the organization that wishes to integrate Melanie? She needs to be placed in a position where her skills can be appropriately engaged. Others need to be sensitized to the potential benefits she offers the organization as well as her personality difficulties. The successful intervention prepares others to support Melanie while empowering her to do her best.

Developing a group strategy in response to the socially inept volunteer or ineffectual leader is often highly effective. This is perhaps the most underutilized strategy in the volunteer sector because it is contrary to the way most not-for-profits function; yet it works well in a number of different situations. It isn't complicated and simply requires a little time. Successful implementation of a group strategy can motivate volunteers to cement their allegiance to the organization and be a catalyst for positive institutional cultural change.

> Successful implementation of a group strategy can motivate volunteers to cement their allegiance to the organization and be a catalyst for positive institutional cultural change.

So how do you initiate a group strategy? First of all, the leader needs to speak to and engage several members of the group and explain the difficulty that is being caused by the inept volunteer. "My friends, we have a situation. Not a problem, just a little irritant that requires your assistance. We have a volunteer with tremendous potential, but one who will require a lot of support. Both of us need your help."

The simple act of trusting others to help in rectifying a problematic situation is empowering. Encourage the group to ask probing questions and to make specific suggestions in order to make the situation theirs. Keep the meeting focused to ensure a transfer of ownership from leadership to the group. Caution and remind the group that this situation is not about them; it's about addressing a difficult situation and avoiding hurting the volunteer's feelings. Engaging a group and elevating its discussion to allow the participants to see the broader picture can save a volunteer and strengthen the organization's culture.

Matthew, on the other hand, might not be salvageable. He operates like a bull in a china shop. He is aggressive, manipulative, and inappropriately lobbies to get his way. Matthew's conniving brings out the worst in people, changes the playing field, and threatens the organization's culture. The group wants to like him because the culture encourages friendships, but the culture of the group also reinforces people taking the high road and extending themselves to one another, and his personal style keeps undermining the organization's core values. A lay or professional leader should advise him that the way in which he deals with people runs counter to the institution's culture and that if he persists in this behavior it would be best for all concerned if he left his volunteer position.

Talking Points

• What is the best way for your organization to work with a misplaced volunteer?

• How do you tactfully uproot and reposition a volunteer?

• What strategies does your organization have in place for dealing with volunteers who intimidate or belittle others?

• How do you develop a strategy for volunteer growth?

• How would you implement a group strategy?

10

WHEN LEADERSHIP
IS LACKING

Addressing a Vacuum at the Top

Effective leadership styles can unite people in common purpose, heal rifts, and create an overarching sense of organizational pride and well-being. If only everyone who aspired to leadership positions had these qualities! Sadly, they don't. Oftentimes, people's group and leadership styles do not mesh with a not-for-profit organization and threaten the health of the culture. Like viruses, if left unchecked, they will spread to others, infecting and compromising the entire organizational culture.

A WOLF IN SHEEP'S CLOTHING

Jules was a vice president in an international volunteer organization. He was corporate all the way. He was recognized by leadership for his abilities, one of which was the way he organized and executed a project. Jules brought to the group a knowledge of how to make use of sophisticated technology and he was able to envision specific results in a way that was a product of the business world from which he came. During his initial years with the organization, Jules appeared to be a well-mannered, thoughtful team player.

While recognizing Jules's abilities, some in the leadership were concerned about his limitations. He was too corporate. He didn't emote. He wasn't a person you wanted to hug. They were concerned that he wouldn't be able to lead well in a volunteer culture.

After several years of watching Jules grow into positions of major responsibility, the senior leadership invited Jules to take part in a mini–think tank. Seven people spent an evening in a board room, drinking coffee and talking about matters of organizational concern. Jules had an idea and aggressively promoted it. Some of the other people in the room also offered suggestions. Jules, seeking to impress the president, swatted them down like flies. Whatever anyone else said was unacceptable. Someone made a naive suggestion; Jules aggressively disagreed, at the same time adroitly belittling him.

Senior leadership was traumatized by the wolf that had been masquerading in sheep's clothing. What was their best course of action?

The following day a senior professional leader, in conjunction with one senior lay leader—both of whom Jules respected—independently engaged him in conversation. The senior professional was direct.

"Jules, your corporate background really showed at yesterday's meeting. It scared the pants off me."

"I thought I was making my point and getting a lot of support from the group."

"No, you were bullying everyone and intimidating the group into silence. Is that how you operate when you sit with the other vice presidents and your president in meetings?"

"Yes, of course it is," he responded.

"Well, what works in the corporate world fails miserably in the volunteer world. How can you possibly expect these people to follow you if you intimidate them? If you were our president—and I hope you will be one day—and you conducted a meeting the way you did yesterday, you would end up a leader without followers. Your officers would simply look at you and say, 'I don't need this crap in my volunteer life,' and leave. You need to lead differently in the volunteer world."

"I behaved like a bully? I just did what I always do at meetings. We all do … aaah," and then he got it.

The lay leader approached him differently.

"Jules, I've been with the organization for a long time. I've seen presidents come and go. I think you could be a great president."

"Really? I'm surprised. I always thought you didn't care about me," Jules responded. "Thank you for those kind words. It means a lot to me."

"It's true. But if you want to succeed with this organization, you need to learn how to handle a group. My God, man, you were like a bull in china shop! You need to make people think that your ideas are their ideas. You have to learn how to guide a discussion, not bulldoze your way through it. Jules, would you like me to teach you?"

And he got it again.

It has taken several years, but Jules has begun to shed his corporate competitiveness when he enters the board room in the volunteer world. Had he not been able to make this transition, his behavior would have put him in an untenable position—in direct conflict with the volunteer culture. It could have resulted in his officers being intimidated and cowed into submission, and the culture of cooperation that thrived on goodwill and consensus could have degenerated into a power-hungry culture in which information was withheld and individual success took precedence over the organization's goals. Instead of the culture of friendship, presidents would view their terms of office as opportunities to rule, not to lead. In the language of the culture, people would once again think of "their projects," rather than team efforts. A negative culture based on deceit could have emerged.

The leadership of volunteer organizations must be able to identify people with potential while being cognizant of their shortcomings. Had Jules not been able to modify his leadership style, a healthy organization could have decided not to promote him to a position of leadership and possibly would have asked him to resign and search for an organization where his volunteer efforts might be better suited.

People from many walks of life seek to climb the leadership ladder in volunteer organizations. Independent businesspeople, government workers, academics, artists, writers, and people from the corporate world all bring their skills to the not-for-profit table. There are times when these skills and ambitions mesh perfectly, and there are times when these people's leadership styles put pressure on the organizational culture. How the organization responds to these potential leaders and their various styles will determine how an organization and its specific culture develop.

> The leadership of volunteer organizations must be able to identify people with potential while being cognizant of their shortcomings.

Each organization's leadership needs to determine if the organization should accommodate itself to a prospective leader's style or if the prospective leader can adapt his or her style to the organization's culture. This is a key question and one that must be weighed by every nominating committee. An error in judgment can result in a disruption of organizational culture. What follows are descriptions of a variety of management/leadership styles that people bring to a not-for-profit organization, each of which represents a unique threat or an opportunity to enhance a healthy and vibrant organizational culture.

THE CHALLENGE OF CHARISMA

Charismatic leaders have the ability to inspire and make it look easy. At times they appear to be larger than life. Often they have the gift to simply reach out and metaphorically touch someone, to move them from one position to another. The world is filled with dynamic leaders. These are men and women who possess a certain amount of charisma and often hold positions of leadership, but they are not necessarily charismatic leaders. The late Rabbi Marshall Meyer, the person who was responsible for the rejuvenation of trendsetting Congregation B'nai Jeshurun in Manhattan, was a charismatic leader. He had a vision and was able to intellectually, socially, and spiritually stimulate others. People flocked to him and hung on his every word. What is the difference between a dynamic leader and a charismatic one? When a dynamic leader finishes speaking, people in the audience might nod their heads in agreement. When a charismatic leader finishes speaking, everyone stands up and volunteers.

Engaging and working with charismatic leadership can be a double-edged sword. If the organization relies solely on the leader's charisma, it can diminish the lay leadership's effectiveness. If the organization seeks to curtail the charismatic leader's influence, the vision can suffer. A proper balance is needed to maintain organizational health.

Charismatic people can also be volunteers. I like to think of this as a Moses and Aaron scenario. Moses was charismatic. He provided the vision. Aaron, the priest, provided the structure to keep it going. Charismatic leaders, whether they are volunteers or professionals, present a challenge to every not-for-profit organization. Organizations are constantly seeking charismatic people to serve as their spokespersons and primary motivators, but charismatic leadership always needs backup, support staff to follow through to provide the necessary structure to ensure success.

THE NEGATIVE CHARISMA VIRUS

Sometimes people rise to leadership positions and have the best of intentions, but because of their lack of skills, their personality, their leadership style, or who knows what, they are abandoned by their support group. This is a case of people with *negative charisma*. It is as good a term as any.

I have worked with three people in my career who exhibited negative charisma. They were conscientious people, active volunteers, who believed in the goals of the organizations they supported. Each of them rose to a level of recognition and responsibility in the organizations of their choice. All of them led successful lives and had devoted families. They were also successful in their professional lives, and in most instances they worked alone.

I suspect one of the reasons each of them became an active volunteer was because they sought the camaraderie they were missing in their professional lives and wanted to feel socially accepted. I suspect that each of them was willing to settle for a certain amount of respect, even though they would have preferred to be thought of as "one of the boys." At times their negative charisma was so intense that all my senses screamed, "Don't interact with them! It's too much work!" I remember how I had to struggle time after time to be patient, to be fair, and to listen. I also remember realizing that if it was difficult for me, it was even more difficult for them. They deserved my respect. Senior leadership can't forget that.

I worked hard trying to integrate these three men into the FJMC. The first two took years. In the third instance, I didn't have to do a thing. It was easy. The experience wasn't emotionally draining, and the person was successfully integrated into a culture of friendship. Why? Because the group understood that the person had a good heart and was seeking friendship. They reached out to him without a moment's hesitation. He never became a leader, but the love and respect he was accorded transformed him into an excellent volunteer— a volunteer who knew he had friends in the group.

> When a dynamic leader finishes speaking, people in the audience might nod their heads in agreement. When a charismatic leader finishes speaking, everyone stands up and volunteers.

THE "I CAN DO IT BETTER AND ALONE" VIRUS

Sheila is a creative individual who understands the not-for-profit culture. She has worked in the not-for-profit world for many years and serves as an active volunteer in a number of organizations. She is a motivator of people, and has experience in the volunteer organization as both a volunteer and a senior professional. She knows how to have fun and how to stimulate others. As a result of her unique skills, Sheila was being fast-tracked and groomed to become the president of a major organization.

In a few short years, Sheila chaired two major committees, and in each instance their portfolios grew under her leadership. With Sheila at the helm, the convention and publications committees were better administered than under the previous chairs.

Unfortunately, Sheila alienated her designated partners by working alone. Conflict and tension arose because of the differences between her style, successful as it was, and the organization's culture, which built strength and leadership through successful committee development. The more the organization's leadership reached out to her and encouraged her to work with others, the less frequently that kind of cooperation occurred.

Senior leadership was concerned. On the one hand, they admired Sheila's creativity; on the other hand, true leadership requires more than creative ability. Senior leadership viewed the way Sheila refused to share information and to engage and mentor people as serious matters that were hindering her advancement. In meetings Sheila emphatically told others what to do, rather than guiding group discussion toward a consensus.

> How leaders respond to volunteers who indicate a desire to resign is always a challenge.

Numerous attempts were made to help her modify her behavior. All of them failed. Sheila was guilty of having the "I can do it better and alone" virus.

Tempers rose, and friendships were strained. One day Sheila called the senior professional and said that she wasn't enjoying herself and wanted to resign.

How leaders respond to volunteers who indicate a desire to resign is always a challenge. Leadership needs to decide whether to take the volunteer's offer of resignation at face value or to view it as a veiled request for more encouragement or recognition.

Senior leadership accepted Sheila's resignation. They realized, Sheila's talent notwithstanding, that people's feelings would continually be wounded by her attitude and approach, and that Sheila would never be satisfied with a position that was anything less than one of senior leadership.

The virus needed to be contained before others adopted her toxic leadership style. It was better to lose one potential leader than to violate and compromise the organization's culture.

Carl was an up-and-coming leader in a synagogue affiliate organization. His corporate background made him a team player. He was a gifted speaker and had a captivating personality. Carl was from a small town, and small town community issues were more important to him than the larger international ones. Over the years Carl rose from chapter president to be co-chair of an international leadership training effort. He was invited to an international board meeting, and while he liked the people at the table and the mission, he wasn't prepared to give the amount of volunteer effort that was required. Carl was placed on another major committee, one that would hopefully meet his needs and at the same time help the larger organization. After a year, he called to resign, saying, "It wasn't fun anymore." Carl liked the guys but didn't identify with the organization's mission. Carl's virus held him back from integrating into the organization's culture. Leadership discussed how to respond to his resignation request. It was accepted.

THE "I CAN DO IT FASTER" VIRUS

This is a minor, less toxic virus than its viral cousin, the "I can do it better and alone" virus. Some people have boundless energy and seemingly limitless amounts of leisure time. They might think faster than most and be able to chair a committee or create an event in a more efficient, more timely manner. There aren't any major reasons why these types of people cannot succeed in the organizational culture. They might require a little mentoring or a friendly reminder to be a little more patient with their fellow volunteers, but people with these qualities can learn to modify their behavior and to fit in and perhaps lead the organization. Initially, the quality of their volunteer work might lack depth, but this can be corrected as well. This virus can disappear over time, and true leadership can emerge.

I'M A LEADER IN SPITE OF MYSELF—SO HOW DO I LEAD?

This situation sometimes exemplifies organizational culture at its best. Not everyone can be a dynamic leader, and leadership styles will always vary. Sometimes people rise to leadership positions as a result of the amount of time they have devoted to an organization or because they reflect the best leadership potential at the moment. They aren't natural leaders, but they are charged with leading despite themselves. If properly supported, they can rise to the occasion, enjoy serving in a leadership capacity, and demonstrate leadership ability. Never underestimate the impact a person in a leadership role can have. The way the position is perceived can carry great weight.

> Not everyone can be a dynamic leader, and leadership styles will always vary. Never underestimate the impact a person in a leadership role can have.

Less-than-dynamic leaders with sound strategies can accomplish more in some instances than a charismatic leader. A person in a leadership position who demonstrates warmth and compassion and is supported by a like-minded group of lay leaders can have a significant impact on organizational growth.

Most of us fall into this category. It's reassuring to know that we have a culture of friends and values to support us. The person who assumes a leadership position and feels supported can serve as a pillar for any not-for-profit organization.

TELL ME WHY I *CAN* DO IT,
NOT WHY I *CAN'T*!

One of the hallmarks of a true leader is the ability to revisit and rethink situations. Bringing together a group of such people can challenge existing structures but will engage, energize, and redirect them as well. Lay and professional leaders need to seek out people who think this way and to create opportunities to bring out their best.

Michael Balkin was the men's club president of Congregation Shaarey Tzedek in Southfield, Michigan, in the early 1990s. We first met when he approached me at an international convention, indicating that he had a concern he wished to discuss. He was convinced that rabbis in Conservative synagogues were not interested in teaching people how to wear tefillin during their morning prayers. He challenged me to do something about this.

I responded that the rabbis were extremely busy and saw the daily service as only part of their overall responsibilities. I asked him to consider if he might be unfairly accusing them of being neglectful. I also asked him what his suggestions would be to address this situation. "After all," I said, "my speaking to one rabbi when a thousand rabbis are equally negligent won't make a difference." He told me that we needed to produce an instructional film that would motivate people to begin wearing tefillin once again. He envisioned this film reaching every synagogue, school, and youth group.

> One of the hallmarks of a true leader is the ability to revisit and rethink situations. Bringing together a group of such people can challenge existing structures but will engage, energize, and redirect them as well.

I agreed and promptly made him the chair of a soon-to-be-appointed committee. We put together a budget; he raised the money and helped other volunteers to develop a marketing plan. Two years later, fifteen hundred rabbis received a flyer promoting the film, and representatives from two hundred congregations viewed the film at an international convention. Michael made it happen. He was motivated, challenged, and provided with the necessary support staff to transform his dream into a reality. The project worked and still works because Michael didn't want to be told why we couldn't make a difference, but how we could.

Talking Points

• How are people promoted to positions of leadership in your organization?

• How does your organization work with people with different leadership styles?

• How can your organization modify the way it operates to accommodate different types of people who aspire to leadership positions?

• How has your organization been influenced by people who have negative leadership styles?

• How has negative leadership affected the success of your organization's efforts?

• What strategies can be developed in your organization to address the complications resulting from negative charisma?

11
Bigger, But Does It Mean Better?
From Independent Minyanim to Cathedral Congregations

I belong to four congregations. Two are in Europe, one is in the city where I spend most of my time and where I raised my family, and the fourth is not far from my family's country retreat. Each of my affiliations connects me to a community. I like the way that feels. The rare times I get to visit the congregations in Europe fill me with a sense of joy and of homecoming. That's pretty much the way I also feel at my home congregation and at the independent minyan to which I belong in the country.

The independent minyan is reminiscent of a *chavurah* I belonged to thirty-five years ago. It is small and intimate. Its atmosphere is informal enough for people to suggest something during the service without giving offense or provoking ire. It functions in exactly the same manner and provides the same sense of intimacy, warmth, stimulation, and community as the *chavurah* movement did so many years ago. The only difference between the *chavurah* of the past and the independent minyan of the present is the name change.

When the *chavurah* movement began in the 1960s, its creators were dissatisfied with the formality, ceremony, and distance of the synagogues of that era. Many independent minyanim are created today for similar reasons. The minyan with which I identify is composed of people who, for the most part, also belong to established synagogues but who still prefer a more intimate and less formal prayer experience.

We meet Shabbat mornings and, since few of us live full-time in this country setting, on occasional holidays in the library of a local Reform synagogue. When the library is unavailable, we meet in someone's home. All of us contribute financially in some way to the host Reform synagogue. Once or twice a year we have social gatherings or hold meetings on a Sunday morning to conduct the minyan's business. Our meetings begin with a traditional egalitarian morning service; men and women wear tallitot and, if they wish to, put on tefillin. The Torah is read in accordance with the liturgical calendar, and it's all followed by a meeting and brunch.

> When a community's needs outgrow the time commitments of its volunteers, paid staff must be brought in and a wholly different volunteer culture emerges.

This is mostly a second-home minyan, though it has begun to attract an increasing number of locals. Shabbat morning draws just enough for a minyan—and sometimes a bit more— in the middle of the winter to upwards of sixty at the height of the summer vacation season. Social relationships have developed as a result of our gathering together, planning services, and sharing responsibilities.

I think it is every Jew's inalienable right to be dissatisfied with the synagogue to which he or she belongs. Most of us in the minyan found that the synagogues in the area didn't meet our needs. After a few false starts, the group coalesced and has been in existence now for several years. The minyan was created to fill a need.

The minyan, like a synagogue, fulfills a variety of functions. Some people attend for social reasons; others seek some form of intellectual stimulation on Shabbat morning. Still others just feel that something's missing if they aren't in a davening community on Shabbat. The atmosphere is friendly, warm, and loose, without the formality of most synagogues. People

I think it is every Jew's inalienable right to be dissatisfied with the synagogue to which he or she belongs. The minyan was created to fill a need.

don't have assigned seats. Some people are not interested in the service and actually bring books to read while the service takes place. Like the *chavurah* of old, people share responsibilities. New people assume leadership positions as required and stay around for as long as the minyan meets their needs.

One summer we attempted to institute a regular Sunday morning minyan for July and August to enable those who needed to say *Kaddish* to do so and to provide the committed daveners with more of the joy of praying in community. It didn't work.

Driving time to the minyan was too great, and people had other commitments. They were hesitant to commit to a regular Sunday schedule. I suspect that was partly because it would have put a real crimp in their Sunday morning tennis games. So the plan died on its own. The community wouldn't support it. As long as the minyan meets the community's needs, it will most likely continue for a long time. Most of us in the minyan are at least forty. Our children are grown, or nearly grown. If younger children were around, the minyan would likely become a synagogue, changing out of necessity its hang-loose identity.

THE CATHEDRAL
CONGREGATION SYNDROME

When a community's needs outgrow the time commitments of its volunteers, paid staff must be brought in and a wholly different volunteer culture emerges. As institutions become larger and acquire staff and maintenance responsibilities, the manner in which volunteerism is perceived and the way volunteers are cultivated change dramatically. Volunteerism is most at risk in large cathedral-like synagogues. I call these buildings cathedral-like because, like Christian cathedrals, they are built to inspire people with a sense of awe and wonder. Tremendous effort goes into their construction with the intent of creating visual beauty and an atmosphere, at least in the sanctuaries and chapels, that fosters prayer and contemplation.

Cathedral congregations are characterized by distance. During services the congregation is physically separated from clergy, who officiate from a stage. This separation is often mirrored by the clergy's and lay leadership's general inability to establish meaningful relationships with many congregants. Certain people are attracted to this type of institution, while others are put off by it.

Volunteerism in cathedral congregations tends to be budget-driven—that is, groups are brought together to do fundraising in order to meet financial obligations, rather than by a need to create and foster community.

The needs and goals of large institutions often conflict with their ability to develop an appropriate understanding of the core values underlying volunteerism. Recruiting volunteers and members tends to be viewed as a means to meet the institution's financial goals instead of a strategy to expand the vision of a community. As a result, the leadership of these institutions (volunteer and professional) generally develops a skewed vision of the nature of volunteerism, undervaluing volunteers and failing to create a coherent plan to attract and engage them.

This skewed understanding is the reason that cathedrals often fail to cultivate large groups of "hands-on" volunteers and tend instead to develop interest-related committees, such as an environment committee or a young adult committee—committees that focus on the needs of special interest groups instead of the larger community. Cathedrals tend to measure congregational activity by the number of people who attend special events—lectures, rallies, concerts, and the like—as opposed to measuring it by the number of people who are actively engaged volunteers.

> Volunteerism in cathedral congregations tends to be budget-driven—that is, groups are brought together to do fundraising in order to meet financial obligations, rather than by a need to create and foster community.

Volunteers in large institutions are generally recruited through bulletins, pulpit requests, or e-mail blasts. This tends to result in a small number of interested people coming forward for limited periods and to take on limited responsibilities, such as agreeing to attend one daily minyan a week or work on a *tikkun olam* project one evening a month. This is a minimalist, passive scenario. Unfortunately, it's one that is adhered to by too many large institutions.

AN ALTERNATIVE VIEW

Another way to attract volunteers is by taking a different approach to the way people are engaged. Cathedral congregations usually attract volunteers by encouraging them to identify with a small group. Small groups make being a member of a large congregation more personal. One of the ways to do this is to introduce a language that unites volunteers under a common banner, even though people volunteer in different areas. For example, if a committee that stresses environmental sensitivity does so as part of a congregational community and as an expression of the organization's broader goals, then it will likely be successful and volunteers will identify more strongly with the organization. If, on the other hand, committee members feel they are functioning more or less independently under the banner of the organization, their loyalty to the organization will be weaker.

> Cathedral congregations have a tendency to attract volunteers by encouraging them to identify with a small group. Small groups make being a member of a large congregation more personal.

Cathedral congregations need to be clear about goals and directions and seek to engage and involve as many people as possible. Unfortunately, it is often far more difficult for large, established synagogues than it is for small, independent country minyanim to provide clear directions and statements of goals.

LOST IN AN UNFRIENDLY PLACE

I was once invited to conduct staff training at a cathedral congregation in a major Southwest city. My task was to teach programming and motivational skills to the staff in hopes that they would learn to be more welcoming. I rented a car at the airport, checked MapQuest, and prepared myself for an hour or so of driving to the synagogue.

The synagogue itself was a long, two-story structure that boasted on one side an airplane hangar–type sanctuary. A group of pre–high school girls wearing uniforms that made them look as if they attended a parochial or private school were playing in a fenced-in playground.

The main entrance was in the front of the building, but the parking lot was in the rear, near the playground. I realized that I had to walk around the entire structure to reach the front entrance. Since it wasn't Shabbat, I assumed that staff, volunteers, the schoolchildren, and visitors would enter through a door somewhere in the back. But the only back door I could find required me to climb a fence. I wasn't about to do that and ended up driving around the building several times until I found a door that looked unlocked. Unable to locate an intercom or buzzer, I opened it and walked in.

Inside were a number of intersecting corridors. I strolled along, passing a number of people performing different tasks. All smiled and said, "Hello." But none questioned my presence or offered to be of help. I wandered past a chapel and a library. Ultimately, with the assistance of a maintenance person, I found the main office.

Suffice it to say that the first item addressed in the staff training was the need for directions and signs. I returned a year later to teach an adult education class there, and was pleased to find colorful, easy-to-read signs throughout the building. This example is more than just a message to synagogues that they should provide simple and clear directional signs. The reason signs did not exist was because the staff knew how to navigate the building, and the synagogue, like a number of cathedrals, was a staff-driven institution. Staff didn't need the signs! Prospective volunteers do. Making your building volunteer-friendly is an initial step toward encouraging volunteerism.

Cathedral congregations consist of multiple cultures that must be united under a common banner and in common purpose. This is a difficult goal to achieve, but language can enable them to do so. Cathedral congregations generally provide a tremendous amount of programming, most of which is staff-initiated. They usually have a host of committees that meet regularly; however, they are rarely united in common purpose and have a tendency to function independently of one another. They're akin to swimmers in a pool, each in a different lane. Too often cathedral-congregation committees only come together to negotiate for space on the community or synagogue calendar. When this reflects the culture, statements like "I'm a social action person, not a young senior person" or "It's not that I'm against them, but we need to schedule the library and they will never give it up" are often heard.

The quality of volunteerism is remarkably different in large synagogues than in independent minyanim. The same may be said for small- or medium-sized synagogues. Each has its own culture.

Large institutions tend to condition staff and lay leadership to seek out volunteers only after specific needs have been identified. Rather than create situations where leadership and volunteers naturally come to the fore, these institutions generally decide that someone is needed to perform a specific task and then seek out a person for the job. This is in part a function of the institution's size and a disconnect between leadership and membership. The professional staff have so many competing demands placed on them that it often seems quicker and easier to simply take on a task rather than to make the effort to recruit and nurture a volunteer.

The situation is further muddled by the belief that programming is the most effective form of membership service. When this attitude is prevalent, it becomes nearly impossible to view volunteer cultivation and leadership development as integral to institutional culture. These perceptions generate a passive, almost negative attitude among professionals and senior volunteer leadership about recruiting additional volunteers.

This viewpoint is easily demonstrated by the way leadership responds to new ideas and new situations. For example, assume for the moment that a synagogue is asked by an outside organization to establish a men's or women's group, often also called brotherhoods and sisterhoods. You would think that professional leadership would understand this as an opportunity to involve more people and give them an added means of Jewish identification. However, if the organization leadership view themselves simply as program providers, then they might consider this offer differently and respond as follows: "What function would a men's group serve?" Or, "We are already using your materials for adult education, social action, the environment, and so on. Look at the host of activities taking place under our roof. Why would we possibly need a single-sex organization?"

> The quality of volunteerism is remarkably different in large synagogues than in independent minyanim. Each has its own culture.

The culture where the professionals think of themselves as service providers fails to understand that it isn't about materials; it is about creating a new vehicle to involve more people, people who, if successfully integrated, would become more active synagogue volunteers.

UNDERSTANDING
THE VOLUNTEER CONSUMER

Leaders need to position the synagogue to attract volunteers. One of the maxims of for-profit organizations is what is loosely termed the 80/20 rule. This means that 80 percent of the work is performed by 20 percent of the staff. A more effective evaluation tool would consider the output of volunteers. Consider an organization's increased productivity as the number of its volunteers rises. Volunteerism can be increased if leaders tailor their products to the consumers and set realistic goals.

This should not be interpreted as a mandate to dilute the synagogue's message, but it should help leaders to develop realistic expectations. Let's say there's a Rabbi Jacobs who boasts that fifteen hundred people attend her High Holy Day services every year. The services are conducted by the rabbi and cantor, with help from the High Holy Day ritual committee. The services are long, and by noon half of the original attendees have left the building. One Rosh Hashanah she appeals to the congregation. She asks that those still in the sanctuary remain until the service concludes. But people are tired and have luncheon invitations or have to get into their cars and travel for an hour in order to visit their in-laws. They simply do not and cannot stay for an additional hour and a half. They have places to go.

Rabbi Jacobs considers herself a successful Jewish professional who fully meets her congregants' needs. Yet she cannot help but feel frustrated when half of her congregation leaves at noon on Rosh Hashanah. In the past she has shared her frustration with the ritual committee, but they have always responded, "What can you do rabbi? The service is the service!"

Perhaps Rabbi Jacob's goal is unrealistic, or perhaps what she's saying she wants is not what she really wants. After all, if she thought about it, she would realize that what she really wants is to have more people come to synagogue on a more regular basis. Once she realizes this, she can construct a plan and might use the forthcoming High Holy Day period as a kickoff toward boosting Sabbath attendance. She might establish additional committees to assist her in this effort or to create focus groups. The result might be a briefer, more meaningful High Holy Day experience, coupled with a growing number of volunteers working with her to increase synagogue attendance the rest of the year, or perhaps an additional separate Rosh Hashanah service that is designed to meet the needs of the group of people who always have to leave.

If Rabbi Jacobs understood her clientele—that is, the consumers' needs—she could come up with a plan that would increase both volunteerism and Shabbat attendance.

Another example: A large North American synagogue, fearful that its membership was being lured away, realized that it couldn't possibly compete with the learning opportunities offered at a major Jewish cultural institution located just four blocks away. It chose instead to focus its efforts on Bible study, basic home and synagogue skills, and engaging entire families in study. In this instance, synagogue leadership wisely understood that, to be successful, it had to address the needs of its current membership and potential constituency. Under the rabbi's guidance, a group of people were trained to offer specific types of service to its members. One group was trained to call every *b'nai mitzvah* family six months before the child's bar or bat mitzvah ceremony and offer to deliver a DVD explaining the Torah service to the family. The film spelled out in a user-friendly manner the choreography of the Torah service, including the proper way to chant the blessings.

The volunteers were trained to use the following language: "This is a service of your congregation. We hope it minimizes the anxiety you might have about being called to the Torah and we hope it maximizes your enjoyment on this very special day. If you'd like an additional copy to send to your family members so they can practice in advance of the date, I would be glad to bring an extra copy with me."

Another group of volunteers was trained to call each family one week after a child was born and invite them, at their convenience, to attend Shabbat services with the baby to receive a special blessing. Even though the male child had a *brit milah*, the volunteers explained that this was an opportunity for the community to formally wish them well.

The rabbi targeted families with children aged nine to eleven and systematically managed to be invited to every family's home, at which time he discussed and offered to teach them how to light Shabbat candles and make *Kiddush*. As a result of these and a few other initiatives, the needs of the community began to be met. Within one year, the nature of congregational activity and participation changed dramatically, and volunteerism rose as well.

THE IN-BETWEEN CONGREGATION

We've looked at independent minyanim and cathedral congregations in some detail. Let's also consider small- and medium-sized congregations; after all, they constitute the majority of synagogues, and they can be special places for volunteers. In these synagogues, people become involved and identify more readily with the community and with its goals. Small- and medium-sized congregations offer a home away from home. They are cozy. In the larger, more complex cathedral congregations, it is more difficult to understand the institution's goals and how those goals can improve the lives of individual members. Life is much simpler in the small-to-medium range.

Small- and medium-sized congregations always seem to need an extra set of hands. They maintain a minimal support staff, which removes overly burdensome activities from volunteers, thus freeing them to market the community's vision. Their budgets are generally tight, often bordering on suffocating. This may be tough on the rabbi and board president, but it means opportunities abound for volunteers to step into the breach. One advantage is that staff and senior volunteers often know almost their entire constituency. Small- and medium-sized congregations are able to focus on specific community and individual needs and, like the independent minyanim, will succeed as long as they continue in this manner.

Like the independent minyan, a small- and medium-sized synagogue provides needed services and offers multiple opportunities for personal fulfillment. Unlike its larger cathedral counterpart, which attempts to offer a complete menu of services but often recruits and retains fewer volunteers, the smaller congregation has a much more narrow focus.

Talking Points

- In what size congregation are you most comfortable? Why?

- What could you do to foster volunteerism in a cathedral congregation?

- If you belong to a cathedral congregation, is the language of your large synagogue sufficiently inclusionary? If not, how would you go about modifying the language to make it more inclusive?

- What are some aspects of independent minyanim that you find intimidating? What are some aspects of independent minyanim that you find especially comfortable and welcoming?

- What aspects of a small- or medium-size congregation do you think help foster a strong volunteer commitment? What aspects of a large congregation do you think help foster a strong volunteer commitment?

• Is it possible to incorporate some of the best qualities of an independent minyan into a medium- or cathedral-sized congregation? How would you do that?

12

WHERE DID THE GUYS GO?

Why Male Volunteerism Has Declined

In 2007, I was invited to deliver a paper at a conference at Brandeis University concerned with the diminishing role of male involvement in Jewish life. It was spurred, in part, by a study indicating that male Jewish teenagers were significantly less involved in synagogue life and had weaker Jewish identities than their female counterparts. In the past decade a number of papers and lectures have been written and delivered on the relationship of religion to gender. Among them is Sylvia Barak Fishman's paper "Matrilineal Ascent/Patrilineal Descent: The Gender Imbalance in American Jewish Life," and a monograph written by Len Saxe with Fern and Ben Phillips ("Standing Under the Chuppah").

Both those works address the "feminization" of the Reform Movement, a reference to the large degree to which women are assuming both lay and professional leadership roles in Reform synagogues and institutions. Almost coincidentally with the publication of the Fishman paper, the Reform lay male organization, Men of Reform Judaism, published *The Men's Seder* in an attempt to involve more men in the Passover experience.

149

The Men's Seder paralleled the large number of Seder experiences created for women in recent decades and inaugurated a series of books devoted to men's needs. Other publishers have also produced books relating to Jewish men, a sign that this is more than an academic debate. The question being asked is this: "Where are the men?"

THE DRIVE TO EGALITARIANISM

The first bat mitzvah took place in 1922, initiating the drive to make non-Orthodox life more egalitarian. This process reflected what was occurring in the secular world, both in the for-profit and not-for-profit sectors. Decades later, when women began to receive rabbinic ordination and assume synagogue leadership roles, some in the Jewish community began to ask whether this change would inevitably lead to diminishing male involvement, whether the synagogue and religious world would remain the last bastion of male dominion, and whether men would remain as committed to Jewish life once women took their place as equal partners on the Jewish scene.

These questions are still being asked. Unfortunately, the only data available on the issue are, for the most part, surveys commissioned by the Reform Movement or information ferreted out from the National Jewish Population Study of 2000. Information about the Reconstructionist and Conservative Movements is anecdotal, since no formal studies have been commissioned.

All the existing studies discount the sociological reasons that men simply are refusing to compete against women in an increasingly egalitarian world—without providing clear alternative reasons for the decline. I believe that the diminished male presence in the volunteer world stems from how the Jewish community has educated men over the past forty years.

FORGETTING THE BASE

For nearly forty years, synagogues have focused resources and programming on empowering women, who for generations were denied the opportunity to an equal Jewish education. This effort unwittingly assumed that men would continue to remain involved and that religious institutions would somehow continue to meet the needs of its male population. It didn't work out that way, and perhaps it was naive to assume that it would. So the drive to empower women in Jewish life has succeeded to a great extent, while the male population was sidelined.

As times changed and generations of male Jews became increasingly assimilated into the broader American community, more and more of them drifted away from religion and the religious institutions that failed to keep up with their changing needs. Relevant and meaningful non-Orthodox synagogue experiences became rarer for men. The secular trend sweeping society, concurrent with feminism's much-needed assault on religious paternalism, compounded the problem. The secular wave is perhaps best illustrated by the 1966 iconic *Time* magazine cover that asked, "Is God Dead?" Within Jewish circles, books such as Richard Rubenstein's *After Auschwitz* challenged traditional religious thought, further contributing to the anti-religious fervor of the era.

Jewish community leaders simply assumed that volunteerism would hold steady through the 1970s, '80s, and '90s, just as it had in the past. It didn't, and Jewish community professionals began to ask, "Where are the next generations of leaders?"

During this period, the "young leadership" effort began to take root. Interestingly, the organized Jewish community (synagogues and federations) was concerned with "leaders," not "volunteers." Community leaders failed to recognize the need to cultivate volunteerism or that volunteerism needed to be taught.

Men and their needs were simply not being factored into the equation of synagogue life. This point was underscored by a conference devoted to "Jews and Gender" that took place at The Jewish Theological Seminary in the 1990s. It was a conference about women. In crafting the conference agenda, it was as if JTS leaders had forgotten that there were two genders.

> More than forty years of neglect has resulted in a disenfranchised male population. To reactivate this population, strategies specifically designed to attract and cultivate men as volunteers and as leaders are needed.

Based on my personal involvement and the anecdotal information of others, I am not sure that male volunteerism and male acceptance of leadership roles in the Conservative Jewish community are still on the decline, but I suspect that neither is it increasing. However, I cannot verify that this is the case since, as I've noted, no formal study has yet been undertaken.

In the Reform Movement, by contrast, studies have have demonstrated that fewer men are assuming volunteer and leadership roles in synagogues. Thanks to the efforts of MRJ (Men of Reform Judaism) and a number of rabbis in the field, an increased effort is currently under way to actively reengage men.

I believe that Jewish men today require targeted efforts to increase their level of volunteerism. More than forty years of neglect has resulted in a disenfranchised male population. To reactivate this population, strategies specifically designed to attract and cultivate men as volunteers and as leaders are needed.

Most men simply do not volunteer. It is a rare synagogue or organization that finds itself with an overabundance of male volunteers. Men usually become involved as volunteers for particular reasons and remain involved because of the nature of what they can gain or, when more altruistically motivated, by what they can give to the group or organization in question. Men volunteer when they have been or are motivated. Women, on the other hand, may volunteer for different reasons, which are outlined in chapter 13.

For a number of years in preparation for the festival of Purim, I would teach the book of Esther on successive evenings to two different groups. On one night I worked with a group of women; the second, with a group of men. We met in someone's home. The story and the scenario were always the same. As soon as I began to teach the women, they immediately engaged. Comments and questions poured out of them. The men took a lot more time and a lot more work.

Men and women are different in so many ways. They interact differently, learn differently, and must be approached differently. So it should come as no surprise that the manner in which they are drawn to volunteering is also different. Men and women may be equal, but in so many ways they are profoundly separate!

This is also evident when working with teenage boys and girls. A number of years ago I devoted a great deal of time to figuring out how I could best teach young Conservative Jews to wear tefillin. After some trial

> Lay and professional leadership need to look at men with the understanding that to involve this population, special positioning, special language, and different marketing are required.

and error, I learned that boys responded better when I spoke of the constriction and muscle tension felt when tefillin are wrapped on an arm. This made perfect sense to an adolescent male whose growing muscles were his pride and joy. Teenage girls, meanwhile, responded better when I pointed out the symmetry and patterns of the tefillin straps when wrapped.

Lay and professional leaders need to look at men as they would all potential volunteers—as participants and potential leaders—but with the understanding that, to involve this population, special positioning, special language, and different marketing are required.

WHAT DO MEN WANT?

Men primarily volunteer for four reasons. Some volunteer because they are searching for camaraderie and gain satisfaction simply by participating. In a transient world in which separation from old friends and family members is the norm and the workplace may be more about competition than camaraderie, creating social networks is difficult. Some men seek to establish these social networks in the volunteer sector. We all need friends.

Other men volunteer to make contacts they hope will further their professional lives. Still others are brought in by a friend or relative, or because their parents, consciously or otherwise, instilled in them the values that foster involvement in community life through volunteerism. Unfortunately, the number of men in this category is shrinking.

Finally, some men become involved because they feel compelled to change the status quo; they want to make a difference.

These factors have to be taken into account when organizing and motivating men. Jewish leaders should create a setting and an environment that enable these needs to be met.

I once participated in a conference call of Jewish outreach workers who were brought together to discuss ways to involve younger men in synagogue life. I was the only man on the call. It was fascinating to hear women say that male involvement would grow if there were more "Daddy and Me" programs—and if their wives told them to go. The conversation reflected the inadequate understanding about what attracts men to synagogue life.

Men in relationships might perform all sorts of activities to placate or please a spouse or loved one. But that does not by any means translate into an emotionally satisfying synagogue experience for a young father. The same experience can be had by taking a child to a park or changing a diaper at home.

I have asked hundreds of men how they organize their leisure time, only to learn that any leisure time they have usually occurs after they've completed a myriad of daily tasks. It doesn't matter if the tasks are enjoyable or simply necessary; they must be completed. Men (not all, of course) tend to be task-oriented. Men make lists and then perform a series of actions to address all the items on those lists. The way many of us accomplish tasks in our personal and professional lives parallels how we function when we volunteer.

> Some men become involved because they feel compelled to change the status quo; they want to make a difference.

Most men are not drawn to and do not seek out open-ended agendas. For them, open-ended agendas, or tasks that go with titles—long-term commitments, in other words—are to be avoided. After all, it's difficult enough to be married or in a committed relationship, raise a family, and make a decent living without taking on yet another responsibility that has no clear end date.

This represents a challenge for synagogues or organizations that are constantly searching for new volunteers and new leadership. Men's clubs and brotherhoods rarely lack volunteers to build a sukkah or run a booth at a Purim carnival. But they have difficulty finding men who will take on the responsibility of becoming an officer, a position requiring a far greater time commitment, and one that may stretch over many years.

CHANGING THE GAME

Reversing the decline of men in Jewish life, and in volunteer positions in particular, will require a multiyear strategy. The model used to cultivate volunteers is effective for both men and women; however, a special language is often required to prompt a man to make the transition from a beginning-volunteer track to a potential-leader track.

It is easy to engage men in short-term activities. Short-term activities are social and provide a welcome camaraderie. Recently, I helped organize two men's clubs in one week. I tried a little experiment: I had one club serve food, beer, wine, coffee, and tea, and I asked the other just to make coffee available and to arrange for the meeting to take place in the synagogue board room. Both groups were demographically and economically similar. It may just have been the people involved, but I found that ideas were more free-flowing when people were placed in an informal atmosphere and setting, something that differed from the workplace.

Men (not all, of course) tend to be task-oriented. Men make lists and then perform a series of actions to complete them.

I once interviewed fifty men's club/brotherhood leaders about what they hoped to achieve during their terms of office. Some indicated that they hoped to increase membership. Others told me they wanted to raise funds for their synagogue or community center. When asked how they would achieve their goals, each responded in kind: "I am going to run programs."

A program is a one-time event. Programs can be owned by one person. In order to develop a more effective long-range view and commitment in men, we need to modify the culture that focuses almost exclusively on a task/program orientation.

This begins by changing the volunteer language and substituting words like "initiative" for the word "programs." A shift in language can successfully change a person's perspective. "Initiatives" continue over a protracted period, often from one administration to another. "Initiatives" keep organizations on track and prevent them from changing focus each time a new person is placed in charge. Men who have been taught to think in terms of "initiatives" begin to understand that the results

> A special language is often required to prompt a man to make the transition from a beginning-volunteer track to a potential-leader track.

of their efforts can have a long-range impact on the organization. The transformation in thinking that results from the change of language strengthens the volunteer's connection to the organization's mission.

THE INTERMARRIAGE CHALLENGE

The Federation of Jewish Men's Clubs created its *keruv* initiative in 1999. In Hebrew *keruv* means "to draw near." In the Jewish world, it refers to outreach to the unaffiliated—or, in this case, outreach to the intermarried and soon to be intermarried—to draw them closer to Jewish living. This initiative was organized as a result of conversations held with twenty rabbis who were invited to observe men's club members and their spouses participating in workshops focusing on different aspects of intermarriage.

The rabbis were asked not to speak during the sessions—just to listen. After the sessions concluded, and the participants had left the room, the rabbis were asked to share their reactions. They were shocked to learn that their congregants were afraid to approach them because they thought their rabbi would be unresponsive, judgmental, and insensitive to the pain they were experiencing.

As a result, FJMC leadership decided to organize rabbinic seminars and create settings where rabbis could learn about intermarriage and discuss their feelings and practices with other colleagues. The leadership also determined that it was important to train strategic partners to work with rabbis in each congregation. At least initially, rabbis were asked to invite men, who were conceptual thinkers and able to present well to a large group to participate in a weekend FJMC training program.

The rabbis had a hard time finding these people. Some of them couldn't. Those who were able to identify participants selected men who had created their own business or were innovators in their fields. Most of the men who were accepted in the initiative for the first four years made a long-term commitment because they were challenged by the situation and wanted to make a difference. Men can be mission-driven as well as project-driven.

> The transformation in thinking that results from the change of language strengthens the person's connection to the organization's mission.

Men and women are pleased when they are thanked for volunteering and are likely to continue as volunteers when they feel appreciated. A successful volunteer experience for a man will also provide, over time, the opportunity for bonding. At times the most satisfying part of a volunteer experience is the few moments of intimacy that occur during or after the work has concluded when participants share a few unguarded comments about relationships and life. For most men, these moments are few and far between in life.

Not-for-profit organizations are constantly searching for men and women volunteers who can go on to assume leadership roles. For this to work, gender-based strategies are crucial. Women and men are simply different.

> A successful volunteer experience for a man will also provide, over time, the opportunity for bonding.

Talking Points

• What is your experience of men in the volunteer world?

• How could a change in thinking about men and volunteerism make a difference in your synagogue or organization?

• Is your organization providing the proper setting to engage men as volunteers?

• What steps might be taken to better engage more men in your community?

13

CRACKING
THE GLASS CEILING

Hearing the Female Perspective

Over the years I've become sensitive to gender nuance. When I taught teenage boys and girls how to put on tefillin, I realized that the language of instruction needed to be different for the two sexes for the act of wrapping to resonate. When I produced the film *The Ties That Bind* and spent several days interviewing women about why they wore tefillin and what they got out of it, I learned that a woman's experience wearing tefillin could not be equated with that of a man. Does that sound sexist? I hope not. Rather, I'd call it a recognition that men and women truly have differing needs.

I interviewed a woman who was in her second trimester of pregnancy. I asked her, as I asked all the women interviewed, why and when she started wearing tefillin. She replied:

> I first began to wear tefillin after I had miscarried.
> It was a terrible experience, and I went into grief
> therapy. It failed. I went to my rabbi and asked her
> what I needed to do to emotionally move from
> where I was to where I needed to be in order to
> cope with my loss. I didn't really expect an answer

but I had exhausted all other alternatives. My rabbi told me to pray every morning wearing tallit and tefillin. At that time we didn't have a daily minyan in my synagogue, but there was one man who prayed in this manner every morning. We arranged for him to come to my house each morning, and we prayed together. After a number of months I became pregnant.

During the course of the interview, I asked her if the act of wearing tefillin had any impact on her soon-to-be-born child. "We resonate together," she said. "When I bind myself to God, I feel my child binding herself to me."

To my knowledge, this was the first new take on tefillin in two thousand years.

I have made a practice of teaching the story of Esther to women's and men's groups each year before the festival of Purim. It is always a wonderful experience. Over the years I've noticed that women consistently respond to the text more quickly than do men. I've also noticed that they are quicker to emote. It takes more time and work to elicit similar responses from the men.

There is a clear difference between prejudice and discrimination based on sex and recognizing that the genders are not the same. Twenty years ago anyone who was working with intermarrieds worked with them as couples. After a number of years counseling this population, I realized that synagogue leaders needed to view intermarrieds both as couples and separately by gender if they wished to integrate them into synagogue life. As my thinking progressed, I added a third level of understanding—that ethnic or religious backgrounds had to be factored into the equation. Communities could not simply program for couples; they needed to understand appropriate gender and ethnic concerns.

This posed a series of difficult questions for a man who had just written a book about volunteer culture and included a chapter about working with men in the volunteer world. What about the women? Stuart M. Matlins, publisher of Jewish Lights, offered me some sound advice: "Find women who work with women and learn what they think. Go out and learn!"

As a rabbi, I have taught, counseled, and worked with women. As a concerned person, I have lobbied for gender equality in the marketplace, but I haven't experienced it anymore than I understood what it felt like to have an unborn fetus move with me as I wrapped tefillin.

What follows are two interviews with women who have devoted a great deal of their professional lives to thinking about and working with women.

Shifra Bronznick is the principal of Bronznick & Co., LLC, a consulting firm that specializes in launching new initiatives and helping not-for-profits navigate change. She has consulted for a wide range of organizations, including the American Indian College Fund, the Public Education Network, the Fresh Air Fund, Hebrew Union College–Jewish Institute of Religion, the American Jewish World Service, the Medicare Rights Center, the Charles H. Revson Foundation, the Nathan Cummings Foundation, United Jewish Communities, and the White House Project. Shifra is also the founder and president of Advancing Women Professionals and the Jewish Community.

Morlie Levin is former national executive director of Hadassah. She has held several positions in the Los Angeles

> There is a clear difference between prejudice and discrimination based on sex and recognizing that the genders are not the same.

Jewish community, including planning and allocations senior associate director and director of the Council of Jewish Life for the city's Jewish Federation. Morlie began her professional career at the Rand Corporation and rose to the level of senior policy analyst. In 1991, she started her own consulting firm, providing strategic support for Fortune 500 companies grappling with global expansion, changing customer expectations, and data overload.

In 1991, she visited Israel for the first time and the impact of that experience led to her active involvement in the Jewish community. While at the Los Angeles Jewish Federation, she launched one of this nation's first Jewish venture philanthropy funds; its work has been nationally recognized as a high-impact vehicle for young donors seeking new ways to engage philanthropically in the Jewish community.

I thank both of them for their insights.

Do you think the reasons women volunteer today are different from those that drew them to volunteer ten or twenty years ago?

Shifra: A number of years ago I did a study of the number of women and the positions they held on boards. I interviewed hundreds of women who sat on boards of JCCs, synagogues, and local federations. After a while it became very clear that women weren't willing to advocate for themselves. Slowly but surely that is beginning to change.

Morlie: No. Certainly not in the Hadassah world, where our founders identified with prestate Palestine and were focused on building a nation. Today when we have the State of Israel, and we have transitioned to making sure Diaspora Jewish women are connected to Israel and their Jewish identity. Hadassah women have always been mission-driven.

Do women volunteer for the same reasons as men?

Shifra: Yes and no. Up until recently—and it is beginning to change—men and women have had different expectations as volunteers. When I first began to investigate how and if women transitioned from local to national leadership a number of years ago, I learned that one of the reasons so few women were serving on national boards or in national positions was a result of how they perceived their impact. Women very clearly need to know that their

> Women very clearly need to know that their activities are having an impact.

activities are having an impact. This isn't always clear in large national and international organizations, and it challenged many women's self-perceptions. They were challenged when they were serving on national boards because it was much less clear how they would be effective.

I believe that men handle these things differently. When I interviewed a whole bunch of CEOs of Jewish organizations, they indicated that when a man would interview for a position he would sit down and ask, "What do you have in mind for me?" or say, "I think I would like to do this." It was very interesting, because I found it occurring over and over again. Eventually, I began to notice that the men would be saying, "What do you have in mind for me?" and "What's next?" and the women wouldn't. As a consequence, the men got the good posts and the women didn't.

Women, on the other hand, generally adopted an attitude that was more like, "OK you're finishing your term of office as president of the JCC. What would you like to be involved in next at JCC?" And they would respond, "It's not up to me." Was it their altruism, or were they conditioned to wait to be asked before they would step up?

Morlie: I think women volunteer and become active because they seek to make a difference. They desire to be identified with a cause larger than their individual interests. I think women identify more readily with a process that leads toward the creation of a policy, while men have a tendency to seek positions where they can make policy.

Do you think women's motivations for volunteering differ from men's?

Morlie: I think both men and women become active for reasons of personal fulfillment, which can have both positive and negative connotations. There are times when both men and women seek volunteer positions for reasons that are less than altruistic, and there are times when they don't. I suspect that the motivations run the spectrum for both genders.

Shifra: I think men and women do it differently. I think when a man does volunteer activity, he is more comfortable doing it and does it for altruistic reasons but also expects to get something back in return.

> I think women identify more readily with a process that leads toward the creation of a policy, while men have a tendency to seek positions where they can make policy.

Men understand that not only is volunteering something to do, but that something comes back through the social networking. I suspect that an innate understanding exists in most men that if it's good for me, it's good for business. If it's good for business, then it's good for me. I think that men feel more comfortable saying, "I know I am doing this altruistically, but I want to get something from it."

I also suspect that women approach accepting volunteer and/or leadership positions somewhat differently than men. Women prioritize their time differently. A lot of times, when women are asked to serve on a board, they will say, "No, I can't do it. I'm too busy with my work and my family." If you ask a man, he'll say, "It's good for my job, it's good for me." I would extrapolate that men are more comfortable with the notion that benefits accumulate through volunteer activity. Not just friendship benefits; there are even business benefits.

Are you saying that men are more likely to seek leadership positions, while women are more interested in positions that provide service?

Shifra: I wouldn't say it was ego. I think men care differently. I noticed it with other issues with my work with women. Men are more comfortable with the "Whatever is good for the job is good for me, whatever is good for me is good for the job" approach. In other words, if you say to a man, "I want you to go somewhere and make a speech," or do this or be on this commission, they don't say, "I have to work." They don't think, "Oh, that's going to be good for me." They have to be really stressed to say, "I can't do it, I have to think about my work or my family."

I think that we think of women as being better at networking. The truth is that men are better at building social alliances because they do it more. It's not because they are socially or culturally better at it; in fact, it might even be more difficult for them, but men just know they have to do it. It's more challenging for women to just decide, "I'm just going to do it." Women tend to consider, and then decide to just hunker down and make sure they exceed everyone's expectations.

What language and actions best motivate women to volunteer?

Shifra: When we visited organizations and interviewed women presidents and CEOs, one thing we learned is that women need to be more hands-on. They needed to see: I do this with my hands this way, and this is the effect. Similarly, women like to be mentored and coached. Women become more comfortable knowing that someone is guiding them. Coaching in a sense is replacing mentoring. It doesn't really matter if the coach is a man or a woman; what matters is that the coach is willing to devote the time and be available. The presence of a coach and the knowledge that his or her actions make a difference actively empowers women.

Morlie: I'm not certain about the language, but I *am* certain that women become active because of the friendships and communities they create and because they understand that through them change can occur. That's why Hadassah women sign up for life.

What is necessary for women to achieve leadership roles?

Shifra: More women today are beginning to realize that if they want a position, if they desire to become a president, they need to make a case for it. They must learn how to lobby and build support groups. They need to get on the phone and call people up, just like anyone else.

> Women like to be mentored and coached. Women become more comfortable knowing that someone is guiding them.

Morlie: Working in a women's organization, it is impossible for me to say that men are more connected to leadership positions than are women. Hadassah volunteers strive for leadership roles within the organization, and I don't think there is a gender difference in terms of interest in leadership roles.

What characteristics are important when targeting and cultivating women as leaders?

Morlie: I think we need to look at women in the context of their situations. When they are young, they need to be engaged in a way that accommodates their stage in life, whether building a career, building a family, or both. As Hadassah volunteers mature and become more involved with Hadassah, their volunteer perspective often expands. As an organization devoted to creating communities of women connected to one another and Israel, Hadassah offers its volunteers opportunities to have an impact in their home communities through study and lobbying on a local or state level. Through that process, Hadassah's volunteers learn the power of leverage and the power of their combined voices.

Shifra: Women need to know they are really making a difference. If they don't know that they are, they might go to the heads of their organization and say, "Look I don't think I'm really helping you. I want to get off the board." For men I have found it to be the opposite. Someone would say, "You know, you're not coming to meetings. I guess you're really not interested." And they would respond, "What are you talking about?" To be a leader in the volunteer world, women need to feel empowered and to know they can make a difference. I think they need to be able to communicate their passion and learn to inspire others, just as men do.

> To be a leader in the volunteer world, women need to feel empowered and to know they can make a difference.

What do you consider to be one of the challenges facing volunteerism today?

Shifra: I think that both women and men want to feel that their work is useful, and I think what you wrote about in your previous chapters is very true. It is an arduous task to use volunteers effectively, and I suspect it is even more difficult for established institutions today. Unlike the Obama presidential campaign, which rallied huge numbers of people for a specific, time-related cause, cultivating volunteers as a tool for institution building is much more daunting.

Morlie: I believe that people need to understand that their lives can be changed, enriched through volunteer activity and that their actions can truly make a difference.

Talking Points

- What is your experience of women in the volunteer world?

- What changes could your organization make that would encourage women to advocate for themselves?

- How does your organization mentor women volunteers?

- What steps might be taken to foster feelings of empowerment and achievement among your organization's women volunteers?

THE NEVER-ENDING TASK

The cultivation and nurturing of volunteers are important and serious tasks. It is my hope that people involved in and committed to not-for-profit organizations have found the ideas in this book helpful as they pursue their professional and volunteer careers. If we wish to build our organizations and our communities, we need to be cognizant of the reasons that volunteers might be hesitant to come forward. We also need to demonstrate our appreciation for the work they are doing. Even though our world is constantly changing, the desire to build communities and make a difference in the lives of others will always remain. Ours is an important task.

> Even though our world is constantly changing, the desire to build communities and make a difference in the lives of others will always remain.

As it says in *Pirkei Avot*: "Rabbi Tarfon said: The day is short, and the work is great, and the laborers are sluggish, and the reward is great, and the Master is urgent" (Ethics of the Fathers 2:20).

SUGGESTIONS FOR FUTURE READING

Peter Block. *Community: The Structure of Belonging.* San Francisco: Berrett-Koehler, 2008.

Bob Burg and John David Mann. *The Go-Giver.* New York: Penguin Portfolio, 2007.

Lee Cockerell. *Creating Magic: 10 Common Sense Leadership Strategies from a Life at Disney.* New York: Doubleday, 2008.

Richard De Vos. *Ten Powerful Phrases for Positive People.* New York: Hachette, 2008.

Martin I. Finney. *The Truth about Getting the Best from People.* Upper Saddle River, NJ: Pearson, 2008.

Rob Goffee and Garreth Jones. *Why Should Anyone Be Led by You? What It Takes to Be an Authoritive Leader.* Boston: Harvard Business School Press, 2006.

John Kottler and Holger Rathgeber. *Our Iceberg Is Melting: Changing and Succeeding Under Any Conditions.* New York: St. Martin's Press, 2005.

Wess Roberts. *Leading Secrets of Atilla the Hun.* New York: Warner Business, 1985.

Mark Sanborn. *You Don't Need a Title to Be a Leader.* New York: Doubleday, 2006.

Paco Underhill. *Why We Buy: The Science of Shopping.* New York: Simon and Schuster, 1999.

Ron Wolfson. *The Spirituality of Welcoming: How to Transform Your Congregation into a Sacred Community.* Woodstock, VT: Jewish Lights, 2007.

Bar/Bat Mitzvah

The JGirl's Guide: The Young Jewish Woman's Handbook for Coming of Age
By Penina Adelman, Ali Feldman, and Shulamit Reinharz
This inspirational, interactive guidebook helps pre-teen Jewish girls address the many issues surrounding coming of age. 6 x 9, 240 pp, Quality PB, 978-1-58023-215-9 **$14.99**
 Also Available: **The JGirl's Teacher's and Parent's Guide**
 8½ x 11, 56 pp, PB, 978-1-58023-225-8 **$8.99**

Bar/Bat Mitzvah Basics: A Practical Family Guide to Coming of Age Together
Edited by Cantor Helen Leneman 6 x 9, 240 pp, Quality PB, 978-1-58023-151-0 **$18.95**

The Bar/Bat Mitzvah Memory Book, 2nd Edition: An Album for Treasuring the Spiritual Celebration *By Rabbi Jeffrey K. Salkin and Nina Salkin*
 8 x 10, 48 pp, Deluxe HC, 2-color text, ribbon marker, 978-1-58023-263-0 **$19.99**

For Kids—Putting God on Your Guest List, 2nd Edition: How to Claim the Spiritual Meaning of Your Bar or Bat Mitzvah *By Rabbi Jeffrey K. Salkin*
 6 x 9, 144 pp, Quality PB, 978-1-58023-308-8 **$15.99** *For ages 11–13*

Putting God on the Guest List, 3rd Edition: How to Reclaim the Spiritual Meaning of Your Child's Bar or Bat Mitzvah *By Rabbi Jeffrey K. Salkin*
 6 x 9, 224 pp, Quality PB, 978-1-58023-222-7 **$16.99**; HC, 978-1-58023-260-9 **$24.99**
 Also Available: **Putting God on the Guest List Teacher's Guide**
 8½ x 11, 48 pp, PB, 978-1-58023-226-5 **$8.99**

Tough Questions Jews Ask: A Young Adult's Guide to Building a Jewish Life
By Rabbi Edward Feinstein 6 x 9, 160 pp, Quality PB, 978-1-58023-139-8 **$14.99** *For ages 12 & up*
 Also Available: **Tough Questions Jews Ask Teacher's Guide**
 8½ x 11, 72 pp, PB, 978-1-58023-187-9 **$8.95**

Bible Study/Midrash

The Modern Men's Torah Commentary: New Insights from Jewish Men on the 54 Weekly Torah Portions *Edited by Rabbi Jeffrey K. Salkin*
A major contribution to modern biblical commentary. Addresses the most important concerns of *modern* men by opening them up to the life of Torah.
6 x 9, 368 pp, HC, 978-1-58023-395-8 **$24.99**

The Genesis of Leadership: What the Bible Teaches Us about Vision, Values and Leading Change *By Rabbi Nathan Laufer; Foreword by Senator Joseph I. Lieberman*
Unlike other books on leadership, this one is rooted in the stories of the Bible.
6 x 9, 288 pp, Quality PB, 978-1-58023-352-1 **$18.99**; HC, 978-1-58023-241-8 **$24.99**

Hineini in Our Lives: Learning How to Respond to Others through 14 Biblical Texts and Personal Stories *By Norman J. Cohen* 6 x 9, 240 pp, Quality PB, 978-1-58023-274-6 **$16.99**

Moses and the Journey to Leadership: Timeless Lessons of Effective Management from the Bible and Today's Leaders *By Dr. Norman J. Cohen*
6 x 9, 240 pp, Quality PB, 978-1-58023-351-4 **$18.99**; HC, 978-1-58023-227-2 **$21.99**

Self, Struggle & Change: Family Conflict Stories in Genesis and Their Healing Insights for Our Lives *By Norman J. Cohen* 6 x 9, 224 pp, Quality PB, 978-1-879045-66-8 **$18.99**

The Triumph of Eve & Other Subversive Bible Tales *By Matt Biers-Ariel*
5½ x 8½, 192 pp, Quality PB, 978-1-59473-176-1 **$14.99**; HC, 978-1-59473-040-5 **$19.99**
(A book from SkyLight Paths, Jewish Lights' sister imprint)

The Wisdom of Judaism: An Introduction to the Values of the Talmud
By Rabbi Dov Peretz Elkins
Explores the essence of Judaism. 6 x 9, 192 pp, Quality PB, 978-1-58023-327-9 **$16.99**
 Also Available: **The Wisdom of Judaism Teacher's Guide**
 8½ x 11, 18 pp, PB, 978-1-58023-350-7 **$8.99**

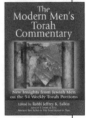

Or phone, fax, mail or e-mail to: **JEWISH LIGHTS Publishing**
Sunset Farm Offices, Route 4 • P.O. Box 237 • Woodstock, Vermont 05091
Tel: (802) 457-4000 • Fax: (802) 457-4004 • www.jewishlights.com
Credit card orders: **(800) 962-4544** (8:30AM–5:30PM ET Monday–Friday)
Generous discounts on quantity orders. SATISFACTION GUARANTEED. Prices subject to change.

Congregation Resources

Inspired Jewish Leadership: Practical Approaches to Building Strong Communities
By Dr. Erica Brown
6 x 9, 256 pp, HC, 978-1-58023-361-3 **$24.99**

Becoming a Congregation of Learners: Learning as a Key to Revitalizing
Congregational Life *By Isa Aron, PhD; Foreword by Rabbi Lawrence A. Hoffman*
6 x 9, 304 pp, Quality PB, 978-1-58023-089-6 **$19.95**

Finding a Spiritual Home: How a New Generation of Jews Can Transform the
American Synagogue *By Rabbi Sidney Schwarz*
6 x 9, 352 pp, Quality PB, 978-1-58023-185-5 **$19.95**

Jewish Pastoral Care, 2nd Edition: A Practical Handbook from Traditional &
Contemporary Sources *Edited by Rabbi Dayle A. Friedman, MSW, MAJCS, BCC*
6 x 9, 528 pp, HC, 978-1-58023-221-0 **$40.00**

Jewish Spiritual Direction: An Innovative Guide from Traditional and Contemporary
Sources *Edited by Rabbi Howard A. Addison and Barbara Eve Breitman*
6 x 9, 368 pp, HC, 978-1-58023-230-2 **$30.00**

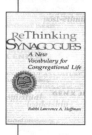

The Self-Renewing Congregation: Organizational Strategies for Revitalizing
Congregational Life *By Isa Aron, PhD; Foreword by Dr. Ron Wolfson*
6 x 9, 304 pp, Quality PB, 978-1-58023-166-4 **$19.95**

Spiritual Community: The Power to Restore Hope, Commitment and Joy
By Rabbi David A. Teutsch, PhD 5½ x 8½, 144 pp, HC, 978-1-58023-270-8 **$19.99**

The Spirituality of Welcoming: How to Transform Your Congregation into a
Sacred Community *By Dr. Ron Wolfson* 6 x 9, 224 pp, Quality PB, 978-1-58023-244-9 **$19.99**

Rethinking Synagogues: A New Vocabulary for Congregational Life
By Rabbi Lawrence A. Hoffman 6 x 9, 240 pp, Quality PB, 978-1-58023-248-7 **$19.99**

Children's Books

What You Will See Inside a Synagogue
By Rabbi Lawrence A. Hoffman and Dr. Ron Wolfson; Full-color photos by Bill Aron
A colorful, fun-to-read introduction that explains the ways and whys of Jewish
worship and religious life. 8½ x 10½, 32 pp, Full-color photos, Quality PB, 978-1-59473-256-0 **$8.99**
For ages 6 & up (A book from SkyLight Paths, Jewish Lights' sister imprint)

The Kids' Fun Book of Jewish Time
By Emily Sper 9 x 7½, 24 pp, Full-color illus., HC, 978-1-58023-311-8 **$16.99**

In God's Hands
By Lawrence Kushner and Gary Schmidt 9 x 12, 32 pp, HC, 978-1-58023-224-1 **$16.99**

Because Nothing Looks Like God
By Lawrence and Karen Kushner
Introduces children to the possibilities of spiritual life.
11 x 8½, 32 pp, Full-color illus., HC, 978-1-58023-092-6 **$17.99** *For ages 4 & up*
Board Book Companions to *Because Nothing Looks Like God* *For ages 0–4*
5 x 5, 24 pp, Full-color illus., SkyLight Paths Board Books

What Does God Look Like? 978-1-893361-23-2 **$7.99**
How Does God Make Things Happen? 978-1-893361-24-9 **$7.95**
Where Is God? 978-1-893361-17-1 **$7.99**

The Book of Miracles: A Young Person's Guide to Jewish Spiritual Awareness
By Lawrence Kushner. All-new illustrations by the author
6 x 9, 96 pp, 2-color illus., HC, 978-1-879045-78-1 **$16.95** *For ages 9 and up*

In Our Image: God's First Creatures
By Nancy Sohn Swartz 9 x 12, 32 pp, Full-color illus., HC, 978-1-879045-99-6 **$16.95**
For ages 4 & up

Also Available as a Board Book: **How Did the Animals Help God?**
5 x 5, 24 pp, Board, Full-color illus., 978-1-59473-044-3 **$7.99** *For ages 0–4*
(A book from SkyLight Paths, Jewish Lights' sister imprint)

What Makes Someone a Jew? *By Lauren Seidman*
Reflects the changing face of American Judaism.
10 x 8½, 32 pp, Full-color photos, Quality PB Original, 978-1-58023-321-7 **$8.99** *For ages 3–6*

Pastoral Care Resources
LifeLights/™אורות החיים

*LifeLights/™*אורות החיים are inspirational, informational booklets about challenges to our emotional and spiritual lives and how to deal with them. Offering help for wholeness and healing, each *LifeLight* is written from a uniquely Jewish spiritual perspective by a wise and caring soul—someone who knows the inner territory of grief, doubt, confusion and longing.

In addition to providing wise words to light a difficult path, each *LifeLight* booklet provides suggestions for additional resources for reading. Many list organizations, Jewish and secular, that can provide help, along with information on how to contact them.

Categories/Sample Topics:

Health & Healing

Caring for Yourself/When Someone Is Ill
Facing Cancer as a Family
Recognizing a Loved One's Addiction, and Providing Help

Loss / Grief / Death & Dying

Coping with the Death of a Spouse
From Death through Shiva: A Guide to Jewish Grieving Practices
Taking the Time You Need to Mourn Your Loss
Talking to Children about Death

Judaism / Living a Jewish Life

Bar and Bat Mitzvah's Meaning: Preparing Spiritually with Your Child
Yearning for God

Family Issues

Grandparenting Interfaith Grandchildren
Talking to Your Children about God

Spiritual Care / Personal Growth

Easing the Burden of Stress
Finding a Way to Forgive
Praying in Hard Times

Now available in hundreds of congregations, health-care facilities, funeral homes, colleges and military installations, these helpful, comforting resources can be uniquely presented in *LifeLights* display racks, available from Jewish Lights. **Each *LifeLight* topic is sold in packs of twelve for $9.95.** General discounts are available for quantity purchases.

Visit us online at **www.jewishlights.com** for a complete list of titles, authors, prices and ordering information, or call us at (802) 457-4000 or toll free at (800) 962-4544.

Inspiration

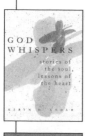

Happiness and the Human Spirit: The Spirituality of Becoming the Best You Can Be *By Abraham J. Twerski, MD*
Shows you that true happiness is attainable once you stop looking outside yourself for the source.
6 x 9, 176 pp, Quality PB, 978-1-58023-404-7 **$16.99**; HC, 978-1-58023-343-9 **$19.99**

Life's Daily Blessings: Inspiring Reflections on Gratitude and Joy for Every Day, Based on Jewish Wisdom *By Rabbi Kerry M. Olitzky* 4½ x 6½, 368 pp, Quality PB, 978-1-58023-396-5 **$16.99**

The Bridge to Forgiveness: Stories and Prayers for Finding God and Restoring Wholeness *By Rabbi Karyn D. Kedar*
Examines how forgiveness can be the bridge that connects us to wholeness and peace.
6 x 9, 176 pp, HC, 978-1-58023-324-8 **$19.99**

God's To-Do List: 103 Ways to Be an Angel and Do God's Work on Earth
By Dr. Ron Wolfson 6 x 9, 150 pp, Quality PB, 978-1-58023-301-9 **$16.99**

God in All Moments: Mystical & Practical Spiritual Wisdom from Hasidic Masters
Edited and translated by Or N. Rose with Ebn D. Leader
5½ x 8½, 192 pp, Quality PB, 978-1-58023-186-2 **$16.95**

Our Dance with God: Finding Prayer, Perspective and Meaning in the Stories of Our Lives *By Karyn D. Kedar* 6 x 9, 176 pp, Quality PB, 978-1-58023-202-9 **$16.99**
Also Available: **The Dance of the Dolphin** (HC edition of Our Dance with God)
6 x 9, 176 pp, HC, 978-1-58023-202-9 **$19.95**

The Empty Chair: Finding Hope and Joy—Timeless Wisdom from a Hasidic Master, Rebbe Nachman of Breslov *Adapted by Moshe Mykoff and the Breslov Research Institute*
4 x 6, 128 pp, 2-color text, Deluxe PB w/flaps, 978-1-879045-67-5 **$9.99**

The Gentle Weapon: Prayers for Everyday and Not-So-Everyday Moments—Timeless Wisdom from the Teachings of the Hasidic Master, Rebbe Nachman of Breslov
Adapted by Moshe Mykoff and S. C. Mizrahi, together with the Breslov Research Institute
4 x 6, 144 pp, 2-color text, Deluxe PB w/flaps, 978-1-58023-022-3 **$9.99**

God Whispers: Stories of the Soul, Lessons of the Heart *By Karyn D. Kedar*
6 x 9, 176 pp, Quality PB, 978-1-58023-088-9 **$15.95**

Restful Reflections: Nighttime Inspiration to Calm the Soul, Based on Jewish Wisdom
By Rabbi Kerry M. Olitzky & Rabbi Lori Forman 4½ x 6½, 448 pp, Quality PB, 978-1-58023-091-9 **$15.95**

Sacred Intentions: Daily Inspiration to Strengthen the Spirit, Based on Jewish Wisdom
By Rabbi Kerry M. Olitzky and Rabbi Lori Forman 4½ x 6½, 448 pp, Quality PB, 978-1-58023-061-2 **$15.95**

Kabbalah/Mysticism

Seek My Face: A Jewish Mystical Theology *By Arthur Green*
6 x 9, 304 pp, Quality PB, 978-1-58023-130-5 **$19.95**

Zohar: Annotated & Explained *Translation and annotation by Daniel C. Matt; Foreword by Andrew Harvey* 5½ x 8½, 176 pp, Quality PB, 978-1-893361-51-5 **$15.99**
(A book from SkyLight Paths, Jewish Lights' sister imprint)

Ehyeh: A Kabbalah for Tomorrow
By Arthur Green 6 x 9, 224 pp, Quality PB, 978-1-58023-213-5 **$16.99**

The Flame of the Heart: Prayers of a Chasidic Mystic *By Reb Noson of Breslov. Translated by David Sears with the Breslov Research Institute* 5 x 7¼, 160 pp, Quality PB, 978-1-58023-246-3 **$15.99**

The Gift of Kabbalah: Discovering the Secrets of Heaven, Renewing Your Life on Earth
By Tamar Frankiel, PhD 6 x 9, 256 pp, Quality PB, 978-1-58023-141-1 **$16.95**
HC, 978-1-58023-108-4 **$21.95**

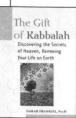

Kabbalah: A Brief Introduction for Christians
By Tamar Frankiel, PhD 5½ x 8½, 208 pp, Quality PB, 978-1-58023-303-3 **$16.99**

The Lost Princess and Other Kabbalistic Tales of Rebbe Nachman of Breslov
The Seven Beggars and Other Kabbalistic Tales of Rebbe Nachman of Breslov
Translated by Rabbi Aryeh Kaplan; Preface by Rabbi Chaim Kramer
Lost Princess: 6 x 9, 400 pp, Quality PB, 978-1-58023-217-3 **$18.99**
Seven Beggars: 6 x 9, 192 pp, Quality PB, 978-1-58023-250-0 **$16.99**